T0144994

Would I *Really* Marry My Cat?!

From the Ridiculous to the Raw,
What I Have Learned about Trusting God
While Living in My Mother's Basement

K.D. Stewart

WESTBOW
PRESS®
A DIVISION OF THOMAS NELSON
& ZONDERVAN

Dedication

To my Lord and Savior,
even when I cried out to You
for release from this season of lament,
You didn't let up.
So I leaned in—to You and to the hurt.
And what I have learned about trusting You,
my good, loving, and sovereign Creator,
is worth more to me
than anything this world has to offer.
From the darkened depths of my heart
that seemed broken beyond repair,
thank You for loving me as You do.

With deep gratitude to my mom,
whose generosity beyond measure
has blessed me beyond measure.
I love you, Mom!

In memory of
Dr. J. Dwight Pentecost (1915–2014)
Pastor, Mentor, Friend
I miss you every day, Dr. P!

Contents

Prologue

I am a single, independent, accomplished, middle-aged woman with a world-class theological education—a Master of Theology from Dallas Theological Seminary, and I'm living in my mother's basement with my two cats.

There. I said it. Or as I often say to my friends who know me and love me anyway, *"I'm living the dream! Living the dream!"* Go ahead and laugh. It's okay. My life over the past few years has required a sense of humor!

If someone had told me ten years ago that I would be back in my hometown of Casper, Wyoming, long enough that I would have to get new license plates and snow tires for my car, I would have found it utterly ridiculous. I am not disparaging my hometown. I loved growing up in Casper. How many places can you live where deer are regular visitors in the yard and wild turkeys are a primary cause of traffic jams? But having spent most of my adult life in southern cities, I am partial to warmer temps and good grits—neither of which are found in abundance in my childhood stomping grounds.

I've always enjoyed coming back home to visit for a week or two. But in the spring of 2012, my "visit" to Casper turned into a divinely-appointed but sorrow-filled furlough that I didn't request and never would have expected. *"Why did you move back to Wyoming?"* I am often asked. The answer is a long and complicated tale that I will share at another time—with the help of the Lord, more therapy, and good meds. But let's just say that my life over the past decade would make for a good movie on Lifetime: Television for Women (Sandra Bullock or Julia Roberts playing me, of course).

My purpose with this book is not to tell you my life story. Rather, it is a compilation of reflections drawn from my season of struggle that are intended to encourage, challenge, and inspire you to embrace this truth: *Life as a Christ-follower is not a "charmed" life. It is a strategically-designed, intentionally-lived testimony of God's faithfulness no matter how things look or feel.* Whether we are experiencing pain or peace, hardship or prosperity, rejection or love, God is worthy of our praise.

Would I Really Marry My Cat?! is just that—praise and worship for my Lord and Savior Jesus Christ. Wrapped in a bit of humor and a lot of gut-level honesty, this book of praise is meant to connect with the heart of the person on the highest mountaintop as well as the person in the darkest valley, or the depths of a parent's basement in my case.

Before I go any further, I need to come clean about the space I have lived in for the past few years. It's not exactly the dingy, dark, depressing downstairs that you might be seeing in your mind's eye. My mom's basement has four bedrooms, two bathrooms, a laundry room, a beautiful patio, and lots of light. It is in no way a dungeon of gloom, and I recognize how blessed I am to have such a bright and spacious place in which to rest, heal, and grow in the Lord. *Thank you, Mom. Your generosity never ceases to amaze me.*

But within the physical walls of the basement is a deep, dark, emotional hole of despair that is furnished with grief, sorrow, fear, and betrayal. And that, my friend, is where I have truly resided for the better part of five years. Fortunately, I haven't lived there alone. When I moved into the pit, the Lord went with me. He didn't take me out of my pain (no matter how hard I cried and whined). Rather, He entered into my suffering, communed with me in my loneliness, comforted me in my grief, and corrected me in my disobedience. *Thank You, God. I am awestruck by Your faithful presence.*

These encounters with the Lord often spill out into my journal, which has grown into a blog for *Deep End Ministries* (TheDeepEnd.org)—the work that God gave me during my season of lament. In the Deep End, we guide Christ-followers well below the surface of Scripture into a never-ending odyssey of God's Character and Truth. Some of my writings in the Deep End are raw. Some are irreverent. Some are humorous. All are *real.* In the pages ahead I hope you will find something that not only tickles your funny bone and touches your heart, but, more importantly, draws you into a life- and faith-transforming understanding of our God, who is always worthy of our trust and praise, regardless of our circumstances.

If just one person is led into a deeper relationship with Christ through these writings, then the years spent in that dark hole—in my mother's basement—in Casper, Wyoming, will have not been in vain.

Welcome to *the Deep End*!

Peace,
K.D.

What I *Didn't* Learn in My Mom's Basement

I am an unapologetic rule-breaker when it comes to literary standards. And for the professional editor or instructor who reviews my work, I am worse than a nightmare in which you marry your cat! (God bless you for your patience, Jenne, Rebecca, Brenda, Lily, and JD). But I am a writing rebel *with* a cause. I only break writing rules when I want something to rise above the average word on the page.

Take the pronoun *he* for instance. Some modern literary manuals dictate that when a pronoun refers to God, it is not capitalized ("he"). I accept that as the norm and make no judgment about it, but, *personally*, I am not comfortable with such standards. In my relationship with the Lord and as I teach about Him and His Word, it is important for me to lift Him up and set Him apart from commonalty.

Other examples of my rebellious writing style include:

- *Capitalization* of words like Kingdom, Gospel, Truth, Creation, Cross, Character, and Name when they specifically refer to Christ's personhood, sovereignty, and dominion. I do this in my writing, but I maintain the capitalization as is in the Scripture translations.
- *Indentation* of nearly all uses of Scripture to set it apart.

- *Verse structuring* in Psalms that reflects the rhythm of these ancient Hebrew songs.
- *Exclamation marks* to reflect what I am actually hearing in my head as the words come out onto the page.
- *Ancient Hebrew and Greek words* have been included in various reflections. While it is becoming increasingly common to shy away from the use of the Hebrew and Greek in popular Christian literature, I feel very strongly that our understanding of God's Word is significantly impacted and even transformed when we consider Scripture within its original language.

For ease of reading, I have transliterated each Hebrew and Greek word into the corresponding letters of the English alphabet. For example, the Greek word for *blessed* that is used in Luke 6:20 is μακάριος (*makarios*), and it carries with it the sense of *happiness*. The Hebrew equivalent, אַשְׁרֵי (*ashrai*), provides further dimension, implying bliss or satisfaction. As used by Jesus in Luke 6:20, *blessed* means "to be blissfully happy, supremely content."

- *Maintaining* LORD *in small caps.* LORD specifically refers to the *personal* Name of God, יהוה (*Yahweh*), which is found only in the Old Testament. When you see this in Scripture references, it emphasizes the promise-keeping nature of God. It is built off of the Hebrew verb *to be*, הָיָה (*hayah*), which God used when Moses asked for His Name in Exodus:

God said to Moses, 'I AM WHO I AM'; and He said, "Thus you shall say to the sons of Israel, 'I AM has sent me to you'" (Exodus 3:14).

So when you see something in the pages ahead that is unfamiliar or doesn't jive with modern literary standards, just know that there is a method to my madness, and it comes from the same heart that ponders feline marriage proposals, singing livers, and stinky feet.

CHAPTER 1

Basement
Reflections
on
Discontent and
Disappointment

Would I Really Marry My Cat?!

Hemmed In

Why Me?!

The Facebook Lie

Poor Christ-manship

Would I Really Marry My Cat?!

It had been a long and painful season of lament during which I lost just about everything—my job, my financial security, my personal security, my home, my community, my dreams for marriage and family, my emotional and physical health, my confidence in the Lord, and ultimately, my peace.

So you can imagine my delight when a new season of joy arrived for me.

I vividly remember that moment—crawling out of a suffocating pit of despair to find myself in a wide open space of hope. For the first time in years, I breathed in contentment, satisfaction, and relief. It was like getting that first whiff of coffee on a cold and lazy Saturday morning.

Then I woke up.

Before I could exhale my bliss gave way to fear and panic.

As I emerged from a bizarre dream, an all-too-familiar sense of disappointment took my breath away. *Would I really marry my cat?!* I shouted deep within my soul.

I know. Ridiculous, bordering on pathological. But at the time there was nothing funny about it. During a torturous season when my sleep was regularly interrupted by hair-raising night terrors, this wacky dream brought a welcome truce with my soul. For the first time in years, I awoke feeling whole. And *that* scared me more than any nightmare I had endured!

You see, one of my lifelong desires had finally been fulfilled. My prince had come. He loved and adored me. He chose me to be his beloved, and he promised to provide for me the rest of my days. This prince looked at me with kind, devoted eyes and said, "Marry me."

And I gleefully accepted his proposal, even though *I knew he was a cat.*

In the dream my friends saw my beloved for who he really was and expressed their horror at my choice. But I didn't care. I could look past the fur and whiskers to finally get what I wanted. What mattered most was that for the first time in a long time (maybe the first time ever) I experienced satisfaction deep within my heart.

Then I awoke, and something dark was exposed deep within my soul—discontentment. *Am I still so fixated on my own desires that I would settle for marrying a cat?!*

By definition, *to be discontent* is to have "a restless desire or craving for something one does not have."[1] What the dictionary does not tell us is that discontentment is one of the Enemy's favorite tools. With it, he can easily manipulate us into choosing the desires of our flesh over God's will for our lives. It's the oldest trick in Satan's book.

> Now the serpent was more crafty than any beast of the field which the LORD God had made. And he said to the woman, "Indeed, has God said, 'You shall not eat from any tree of the garden'?" The woman said to the serpent, "From the fruit of the trees of the garden we may eat; but from the fruit of the tree which is in the middle of the garden, God has said, 'You shall not eat from it or touch it, or you will die.'" The serpent said to the woman, "You surely will not die! "For God knows that in the day you eat from it your eyes will be opened, and you will be like God, knowing good and evil." When the woman saw that the tree was good for food, and that it was a delight to the eyes, and that the tree was desirable to make one wise, she took from its fruit and ate. (Genesis 3:1–6)

Even though God had created for man and woman an exquisite garden that provided everything they needed in *exceeding abundance*, it wasn't enough for Adam and Eve. They didn't know it, but they were ripe for Satan's picking. And the Enemy, who can spot low-hanging fruit a mile away, seized the moment. "God is holding something back from you," the Serpent has hissed into man's ear since the beginning of time.

I am among those who fell right into his wicked trap, which creates disappointment and then turns it into disobedience. For crying out loud, discontentment took such hold of my heart that my subconscious reasoned it would be good for me to marry my cat!

Fortunately, *discontentment* is also in God's toolbox. He uses it to warn of looming disaster. It shows us that our will is not aligned with the Father's and confronts us with a choice: obedience or disobedience? Just think about the impact that unbridled discontentment had in the lives of some of our spiritual ancestors:

- The Israelites were disgruntled with God's provision, even though He had delivered them from the iron-fisted clutch of Pharaoh. Their dissatisfaction led to a forty-year detour in the desert and an entire generation missed out on life in the Promised Land (Numbers 13:1–14:38).
- Ananias and Sapphira weren't satisfied with God's provision, even though He met all of their needs through the newborn church. The greedy pair was struck dead by the Lord for withholding contributions and lying about it (Acts 5:1–11).
- Judas wasn't content with following Jesus, whose promise of eternal life did not guarantee a life of prosperity on earth. He chased after self-aggrandizement and wound up dead, rotting in a field littered with his guts (Matthew 26:14–16; Acts 1:18).

Discontentment. It starts out as a tiny seed rooted in that place in the heart where our dreams live. The Enemy feeds it by convincing us that God is withholding something good from us. Unchecked, it can grow into a weed of restless desire that chokes out our satisfaction with the Lord.

We often hear prosperous people say, "I'm living the dream." But I think it's fair to say that none of our spiritual ancestors were *living the dream*. The life God chose for them included suffering. But those who obediently laid down their own will for the will of God found that the Lord had the better plan for their lives all along.

What about you? Are you perfectly content with your life? Is it all going the way you planned and hoped? If it is, praise God! But if it isn't, can you also praise God? I would never have written my life story the way it has played out. But thanks be to God that I am not the author of my life and I am not living the dream, or I just might be hitched to a feline!

Lord, hear my prayer.
Mercifully expose discontentment in my heart
before it leads to disobedience in my relationship with You.
You are my Father.
And no good father withholds from his children
that which he knows is best for them.
You are a good Father. You are a faithful and loving Father.
You are the One and Only Perfect Father.
Help me to reject the hissing lie of the Serpent
and trust that, no matter my circumstances,
You will provide for my needs, often in exceeding abundance.
Help me to be satisfied in being Your beloved child.
What more could I really ask for?
For the honor and glory of Jesus Christ, Your Son and my Savior.
Amen.

Hemmed In

In the mid-1990s I called Tucson, Arizona, home. I thought I hit the jackpot when I was hired as a TV news anchor and reporter in the "Old Pueblo." Tucson's glorious sunsets, warm temperatures, and *no snow* held great appeal for me—for about six months. Then I discovered that scorpions in my bed and javelinas (wild pigs) on my porch made for a less-than-hospitable environment. Not to mention the blistering heat that literally melted the makeup off my face during my live shots. People are quick to say, "But it's a dry heat." Well for me, 120+ degrees of *any* kind of heat is beyond tolerable!

I lived in Tucson for five years, but it felt like an eternity. The last three of those years, discontentment was my significant other. I did everything I could to move on, including hiring two of the best agents in the TV news business. But no doors would open. It was as if I had been locked in by someone from the outside (besides the wild pigs who camped out on my doorstep).

> You have enclosed me behind and before,
> And laid Your hand upon me. (Psalm 139:5)

Whenever life feels like it is closing in on me and those old feelings of being locked into my life circumstances resurface, the Lord takes me to Psalm 139—one of the most beautiful songs in the entire Psalter.

O Lord, You have searched me and known me.
You know when I sit down and when I rise up;
You understand my thought from afar.
You scrutinize my path and my lying down,
And are intimately acquainted with all my ways.
Even before there is a word on my tongue,
Behold, O Lord, You know it all.
You have enclosed me behind and before,
And laid Your hand upon me.
Such knowledge is too wonderful for me;
It is too high, I cannot attain to it. (Psalm 139:1–6)

Nestled within this exquisite Hebrew worship song about the Lord's omniscience (all-knowing) and omnipresence (present everywhere) is verse 5, a verse that at first glance seems to emphasize the softness of God's sovereignty.

You have enclosed me behind and before,
And laid Your hand upon me. (verse 5)

I have long viewed verse 5 as something akin to a warm blanket wrapped around me by the Lord to protect me from the cold world. But in the Ancient Hebrew this verse is about as warm and fuzzy as a battering ram. The Hebrew root of *enclosed* or *hemmed in*, מָצוֹר (*matsor*), is a military term that means "to relentlessly attack an opponent's stronghold."[2] In the Ancient Near East, an enemy army would conquer a city by first surrounding it, then cutting off all supplies to the inhabitants, and finally using battering rams to breach the city walls. For those trapped inside, there was no escape. The only way to survive was to surrender.

So in Psalm 139, when we read "You have enclosed me behind and before, and laid Your hand upon me," it does not mean that the Lord is swaddling us like fragile babes. It means He has us surrounded on all sides, leaving no way of escape from His will. When we feel trapped by life's circumstances, our only viable option is to *surrender* to the Author of our lives.

Ultimately, I did move on from Tucson. But thanks be to God, it was in His time and not mine. You see, my Grandma Jo was dying during those last three years of my time in Arizona. She and my Grandpa Stu lived near Phoenix. And just about every weekend, I would make the two-hour journey to love on both of them. I can still see the delight in Grandma Jo's weary eyes when I walked through the door. I can still feel her frail hands, knotted with arthritis, that seemed to sigh in relief as I massaged and manicured them. And I can still hear her licking her lips when I made soup for dinner.

My senses came alive as I ministered to my dying grandmother. And I wouldn't trade that time or those memories for anything, not even for an escape from the misery of Tucson. Several months after Grandma Jo went to Heaven, I landed a new job in Atlanta, Georgia, and I was never happier. I'm certain the timing was not coincidental.

Are you feeling "enclosed" or "hemmed in" by life's circumstances right now? Maybe it's a difficult relationship or an illness that has you feeling trapped. Could it be that your debt has you pinned to the mat or that you have found yourself in a seemingly dead-end job?

The truth is, you just might be trapped—by your Creator. And it's not because He's cruel or can't see your struggle. The God who knit you together in your mother's womb (Psalm 139:13) has purpose for your life, even in seasons of misery. Like a military general lays siege to a city, He has you surrounded. You can try and fight your way out of your circumstances like I did. But I've learned that surrender is a far better response. It may not free us from our struggles any sooner, but surrender does free us to live peacefully in the midst of God's will.

Such knowledge is too wonderful for me. (Psalm 139:6)

Creator God,
When life gets tough,
my instinct is to panic and look for a way out.
I am so quick to become discontent with the life You have given me.
Help me to adjust my auto-pilot response from panic to peace,
knowing You are in control of my circumstances.
As painful or difficult as they may be,
there is purpose in my struggles, and it is good.
Thank You for loving me enough to keep me hemmed in.
For the honor and glory of Christ Jesus.
Amen.

Why Me?!

The church was reserved. The dress perfectly altered to fit her like a glove. The invitations were in the mail, and she could almost taste the cake that would represent such a sweet start to her happily-ever-after. In just a matter of days, this beautiful young woman would become a blushing bride, a Mrs. to the Mr. who had swept her off her feet and pledged his everlasting love to her. And then—out of the "something blue"—he backed out. Every bride's worst nightmare. Her groom ditched her! Suddenly her happily-ever-after turned into happily-*never*-after.

"Why me?" the young woman asked her mom.

As the mother of the bride-*not*-to-be fumbled for the right words of comfort, her daughter interrupted. "No, Mom, not why did I have to be the girl whose groom ran away?" It wasn't being jilted that puzzled her. It was God's grace that astounded her! "Why did the Lord save me from walking down the aisle into a bad marriage?" With so many broken marriages in the world, she wondered why God spared her from such heartache in the future.

Wow! I'll bet you didn't see that coming, did you? Neither did her parents as they marveled at their daughter's spiritual maturity and confidence in her Creator. This is the true story of friends of my family, and we were all awed by how beautifully this young woman handled the disappointment. When the pain of rejection could have (in so many of us *would have*) won the day, she demonstrated wisdom and grace far beyond her years.

Pause for a moment and just think about that. Put yourself in her place and ponder how you would respond. We would all like to think we have that kind of spiritual maturity. But I'll be honest with you. I don't think I would have taken the blow nearly as graciously. In fact, I probably would have turned into bridezilla-gone-wild on anyone who even suggested that I should rejoice in the moment. And you know what? I think God would be okay with that, as long as I pressed into the pain until it became praise.

It can be a long and difficult journey from self-pity to praise. And most of God's people have to traverse it at some point or another, including the heroes of our faith. At a time of pulverizing disappointment, even King David—a man after God's own heart—raged at the Lord before he recognized God's sovereignty and worshipped Him for His faithfulness, even in the midst of despair.

For the choir director. A Psalm of David.

How long, O LORD? Will You forget me forever?
How long will You hide Your face from me?
How long shall I take counsel in my soul,
Having sorrow in my heart all the day?
How long will my enemy be exalted over me?

Consider and answer me, O LORD my God;
Enlighten my eyes, or I will sleep the sleep of death,
And my enemy will say, "I have overcome him,"
And my adversaries will rejoice when I am shaken.

But I have trusted in Your lovingkindness;
My heart shall rejoice in Your salvation.
I will sing to the LORD,
Because He has dealt bountifully with me. (Psalm 13)

The circumstances behind Psalm 13—David's quintessential lament psalm—are not clear. But the agony is evident. In the first two verses, David throws a huge pity party for himself, literally accusing God of abandoning him. But drop down to verses 5–6. What does David do? He *praises* the Lord for His faithfulness.

What happens that causes David to move from self-pity to praise?

Look at verse 3. David asks the Lord to "enlighten" his eyes. He may be alluding to his experiences on the battlefield when he held his own men in his arms as they died, as the light went out in their eyes. David is in so much pain (physical and emotional) that he literally feels like he's going to die, that the light will go out in his eyes. So he asks the Lord to give him a different perspective on his situation. David wants to see things the way God sees them. When he receives a new, more spiritually mature view of his struggle, he responds with trust and confidence in the Lord.

"Why me?" In the midst of suffering, it is difficult to see God's purpose. But when we ask the Lord for new perspective—His perspective—the "why me?" doesn't reflect self-pity. Rather, it is spoken with a sense of blessing. We may not know how or when our suffering will end. But we can be certain that the One who brings life from death will bring His glory and honor out of our struggles. When we make that journey from pity to praise, and trust in Him, we are able to stand in awe and not disappointment of God's sovereignty.

Sovereign God,
Forgive me for all the times I have cried out with anger,
"Why me?!"
Thank You for Your patience
as I make the journey from pity to praise.
And thank You, Lord, for those saints who have gone before me
on that journey and lived to tell about it.
How grateful I am for the encouraging witness of King David,
as well as this wise young bride.
Let me be an encouragement to others
as we all navigate the disappointments of life.
I love You, Lord.
In Jesus' mighty Name and for His glory.
Amen.

The Facebook Lie

Have you ever fallen for the Facebook lie? No, not the way people misrepresent themselves on Facebook (although that is a huge trap in and of itself). I'm talking about a far more insidious lie, a spiritual parasite that burrows into your heart, feeds on your peace, and produces nothing but discontent and depression.

Look at that family! They all love each other so much.
Wish I had a family who all got along like that.
Wow! Now that is the way to do a vacation!
I'll never be able to afford such a great getaway.
Engaged! My friend is getting married!
I'm so lonely. Will it ever be my turn?
They just moved into their dream home!
Why is their life a dream and mine a nightmare?

For years sociologists have studied the connection between Facebook and mental health issues like depression, hopelessness, and low self-esteem. But a recent study published in the *Journal of Social and Clinical Psychology* made a groundbreaking conclusion regarding the connection between depression and Facebook. "Our study is the first of its kind to determine that the underlying mechanism between this association is social comparison. In other words, heavy Facebook users might be comparing themselves to their friends, which in turn, can make them feel more depressed," explained the study author in a *Forbes* article.[3]

Before you say, "Duh!" to the incredibly astute (and probably exceedingly costly) conclusion that we can get really depressed when we compare ourselves to our Facebook friends, let me offer a different thought on the so-called "underlying mechanism" of the Facebook blues.

When we see something we want but can't or don't have, we feel cheated or deprived. And it's a short leap from feeling deprived to acting depraved.

> Now Sarai, Abram's wife had borne him no children, and she had an Egyptian maid whose name was Hagar. So Sarai said to Abram, "Now behold, the LORD has prevented me from bearing children. Please go in to my maid; perhaps I will obtain children through her." And Abram listened to the voice of Sarai. (Genesis 16:1–2)

Even though God had *vowed* to give Abram and Sarai (later renamed Abraham and Sarah) a son, Sarai's impatience fueled her disappointment in the Lord, who was apparently taking too long to deliver on His promise. So, she took a shortcut and told her husband to conceive a child with her maid. It never ceases to amaze me what we are willing to do to get what we want.

The "underlying mechanism" that connects depression and Facebook is not "social comparison." It is disappointment in the Lord! We see others' blessings and question God's love for us and His will for our lives. Our unbelief bottoms out in depression when we look at others and think we've been cheated by God.

Have you ever fallen for the Facebook lie? I have—more than once! In fact, there have been times when I have blocked friends' happy posts, because I just couldn't stomach one more wedding picture or baby announcement or happy family photo. I don't begrudge any of my Facebook friends those things. I just didn't want to hear about their happiness, because it made me feel deprived of my own dreams. How twisted is that?

It's about as twisted as a group of folks who, after being miraculously delivered by the Lord from the oppression and slavery of the king of Egypt, begged God to put them back under the rule of a king in the Promised Land. Everyone else in their Ancient Near Eastern neighborhood got to have human kings. Why couldn't they? Think about it. The people who were hand-picked by the King of Kings to represent Him on earth felt cheated because He didn't give them what other people had—an earthly king.

> "Thus says the LORD, the God of Israel, 'I brought Israel up from Egypt, and I delivered you from the hand of the Egyptians and from the power of all the kingdoms that were oppressing you.' But you have today rejected your God, who delivers you from all your calamities and your distresses; yet you have said, 'No, but set a king over us!'" (1 Samuel 10:18–19)

As we read in 1 Samuel 9–10, God conceded to Israel's demands and allowed the nation to choose who they believed would better serve them. Their choice: Saul. Their selection process: a beauty pageant! Saul got the people's vote because he was the tallest, best-looking man among them (1 Samuel 9:1–2). As it turned out, those were his finest qualities. Saul went down in the history books as one of the most wicked and cowardly kings of all time.

Are you restless for God's blessings? Rest assured that there are no limits to His love and faithfulness. The Enemy would have you believe that by the time "your turn" comes around, the Lord will have used up all of His blessings on everyone else. That's a lie. The truth is, there aren't enough Facebook posts to capture even a small measure of God's goodness. And you and I can have no better "friend" than the One who died on the Cross for us—the One who rose from the dead and sits at the right hand of the Father, defending us.

I *like* that truth and am grateful to be able to *forward* it with you. Let's go viral with it!

Father God,
Forgive me for being disappointed in You.
I have allowed that disappointment
to go viral in my head and heart,
and the result is always depression.
You are the Author of my life,
and I look forward to reading the last chapter
in Your Presence.

Then it will all make sense.
But until then, Lord,
give me the strength to reject the lies of the world.
Instead, help me to embrace and forward
the truths of Your Word
that can be blocked but never deleted.
Thank You for loving me first,
so I could love and know You.
In the Name of Your Son, Jesus Christ,
my Truth, my Hope, My Joy, My Savior.
Amen.

Poor Christ-manship

By his own admission, Carolina Panthers quarterback, Cam Newton, is an outspoken, evangelical Christian athlete. To his credit, he has not shied away from giving God the glory for his successful football career. During the pregame show before Super Bowl 50, he even starred in a commercial that offered this prayer: "I know You molded me different. You placed purpose on my shoulders. So now I come to You, loyal. Give me the strength to finish this, my way."

But when things didn't go Cam's way in the big game against the Denver Broncos, the NFL MVP behaved like a pouting toddler. Shrouded in a black hoodie, he brooded his way onto a press platform after the defeat, mumbled through a few questions with pathetic two-word answers, and then stormed off.

The public beating he took for that performance may be even worse than the shellacking he took from the Broncos' defensive line! Pro Football Hall of Famer Deion Sanders kicked off a wave of criticism, saying to Cam Newton, "You are the face of our brand right now, you can't do that."[4] Truer words could not be spoken.

Brand awareness is everything when you represent, not just in the NFL, but more importantly, the church. And on a worldwide platform, Cam Newton lost that brand awareness, completely forgetting about Who he ultimately represents.

I don't want to pile on the guy. He got plenty of that from other players, commentators, the media, and probably worst of all, his mom, who texted this reminder to him before the game: "I want you to understand that hot and cold water comes out of different fountains. You are either hot or cold. You have a big platform. Which fountain are you? ... *Thru your language and actions, speak words to uplift and not tear down. ... You win with your character and powerful words that you speak. Cam, you are highly favored. God is on your side. ... Remember God!*" (Emphasis mine.)[5]

Well, Mom, Cam forgot.

But haven't we all in the midst of disappointment? I am guilty of countless pity parties and conniption fits with the Lord when I haven't gotten my way. In fact, I would bet every Christ-follower on the planet has stomped his or her foot at least once in anger with the Lord regarding life circumstances. Not surprisingly, God has something to say about that.

> Better to be slow to anger than to be a mighty warrior,
> and one who controls his temper is better than one
> who captures a city. (Proverbs 16:32 NET)

For Cam Newton, Solomon's wise advice might be translated this way: It takes more courage and discipline to be the humble loser in the locker room than to be the MVP still celebrating on the field. The quarterback who can hold his tongue in the face of disappointment is more impressive than the quarterback who is holding the Lombardi Trophy.

But whether we are multimillion-dollar athletes, stay-at-home moms, presidential candidates, mid-level managers, Hollywood stars, or minimum-wage fast-food employees, God expects the same from *all* of His people—humility. That is the gold standard of the Lord, and it comes through spiritual discipline. It is cultivated by being rooted in the Lord, centered in His Word, and accountable to other believers who aren't afraid to tell us when we're out of line (Keep preaching it, Deion Sanders!). And the greatest test of humility doesn't come with a win. It is best exhibited in a loss, when we praise the Lord for His faithfulness despite our disappointment.

I pray that Cam Newton has gained some spiritual maturity and discipline through his Super Bowl loss. And I hope that one day the Lord might even give this incredibly talented athlete another shot at praising Him from a worldwide platform, to revise his original pregame prayer to "Give me the strength to finish this, *Your* way." But even if Cam doesn't learn one thing from his demonstration of poor Christ-manship, I know I have. I hope you have too. Every day, let's take the field prepared to praise God—win or lose.

Lord,
I love You and want so much to represent You well.
You teach us that to seek Your glory,
we need to seek Your will, not our own.
In our prideful flesh that's hard under any circumstances,
and especially when faced with crushing disappointment.
By Your Spirit, give me the humility
to willingly set aside my will for Your will each and every day.
And, Lord, as I seek to grow my faith and relationship with You,
I pray that one day my will will be Your will.
In Christ's Name and for His glory and honor.
Amen.

CHAPTER 2

Basement Reflections
on
Fear

I Ain't No Grasshopper!

"You're in my seat!" I said to the little grasshopper who had chosen my favorite patio chair for his afternoon nap. You would think that a giant talking head with a mouthful of teeth and a loud voice would be enough to cause any little critter to jump. But not this guy. He got there first and wasn't going to budge.

Now, I don't have anything against grasshoppers. I didn't want to kill or even hurt the little guy. I just wanted him to move! So I gave him a little flick and sent him packing. Moments later, as I settled in to enjoy a beautiful summer afternoon on the patio, guess who decided to join me on my chair? *"Seriously?* Who do you think you are?" I snapped at the tiny, green twerp. Though I don't speak bug language, I'm pretty certain he snapped back, "Well, I ain't no grasshopper!"

Nearly knocking me (not the insect) out of my chair with laughter, the Lord brought to mind a story I had just read in the book of Numbers. (Contrary to popular belief, Numbers is not just a boring record of one genealogy after another. It is a fascinating account of the Israelites' journey from Egypt to the Promised Land). In Numbers 13, we read about the Israelite spies who were sent into the Promised Land on a reconnaissance mission.

> Then the Lord spoke to Moses saying, "Send out for yourself men so that they may spy out the land of Canaan, which I am going to give to the sons of Israel." … When Moses sent them to spy out the land of Canaan, he said to them, "Go up there into the Negev; then

go up into the hill country. See what the land is like, and whether the people who live in it are strong or weak, whether they are few or many. How is the land in which they live, is it good or bad? And how are the cities in which they live, are they like open camps or with fortifications? How is the land, is it fat or lean? Are there trees in it or not? Make an effort then to get some of the fruit of the land." (Numbers 13:1–2, 17–20)

Unexplored territory. Most of us have had to face it—standing there with our heels settled into the comfort of familiarity and our toes touching the horizon of uncertainty and fear. It can be an exhilarating time filled with the thrill of adventure and the hope of what lies ahead. But rarely does it come without at least a bit of trepidation.

Not too long ago, my two oldest nieces left the nest and headed off to college—one to Colorado in pursuit of her dream to be a doctor and the other to Missouri in pursuit of her dream to be an Olympian. I am so excited for both them, for the thrill and adventure of exploring the new territory that awaits each of them. But I also see in their eyes (eyes that I have looked into since they were just days old) real *fear*—fear of life on their own for the first time, fear of the unknown, fear of being separated from family and friends, fear that things might not turn out as they had hoped, and fear that they will disappoint those who have loved and encouraged them.

Aside from the usual "I love you" and "I miss you" and "I'm praying for you!" I want to give them some little nugget of wisdom that they can tuck away in their hearts for those times when they need a bit of encouragement. And my little, green-winged, courageous patio companion has given me the answer: "Don't be a grasshopper!"

As the story continues in Numbers 13:25–33, the Israelite spies obediently ventured into the unknown territory—the Promised Land. And just as the Lord had promised, it was flowing with milk and honey! An expanse of abundance was theirs for the taking.

But they found something else as well.

"The people who live in the land are strong, and the cities are fortified and very large." ... "We are not able to go up against the people, for they are too strong for us." So they gave out to the sons of Israel a bad report of the land which they had spied out, saying, "The land through which we have gone, in spying it out, is a land that devours its inhabitants; and all the people whom we saw in it are men of great size." (Numbers 13:28, 31–32)

Just imagine the terror twisting their faces and swelling their eyes! Scary enough to convince the entire nation of Israel (hundreds of thousands of people) to stay in the barren, lifeless wilderness rather than enter the land flowing with milk and honey. God had promised the land to them (Exodus 3:17). And the people had clear evidence that the Lord could be trusted. He parted the Red Sea and rescued them from Egypt for crying out loud! So they should have trusted that God would deal with any and all threats in the Promised Land, including giants.

But, oh, the power of fear! When it becomes a giant in our hearts, we— the image bearers of the Creator of the Universe—become like pitiful, little bugs in our own eyes and in the eyes of the world. Pause for a moment, and let the confession of the Israelite spies sink in.

We became like grasshoppers in our own sight, and so we were in their sight. (Numbers 13:33)

Fear shrinks faith, not only in our own eyes but also in the eyes of the Enemy.

"Don't be grasshoppers!" I say to my precious nieces and to all of us who have put our trust in the Lord. Not as a boost of confidence in our human strength, but as a boost of confidence in the power of our Savior— who gave His life for us, rose from the grave and sits at the right hand of the Father to defend us, promises to *never* leave us or forsake us, and will be waiting for us just over the horizon when we leave this earthly adventure behind and step (not hop) into the ultimate Promised Land.

Oh Lord my God,
Nothing in all of Creation can compare
to Your power, sovereignty, and love.
You spoke this world into existence
and knit me together in my mother's womb.

And by the blood of Your Son,
You have claimed me as Your daughter.
So why in the world would I let
anything or anyone come before You?
And yet, I do.
Often, the thing that gets the best of me is fear.
There are giants in my land.
Forgive me Lord for not trusting in You
to walk with me through any and all circumstances.
By Your Spirit,
enable me to see myself not as a grasshopper
but as a daughter of the King of the Universe,
Who has promised to never leave or forsake me.
I love You Lord, and I am so grateful to be Your daughter.
In the Name of Your Son, Jesus Christ,
my Savior and giant-slayer.
Amen.

No, No! Not That!

It's one of America's favorite summer pastimes, the garage sale, where one man's trash becomes another's treasure. Every summer weekend, in just about every community across the United States, garage sale signs pop up and point the way to prize finds that you can get for pennies on the dollar.

After several years of acquiring significant inventory, it was my family's turn to sell our stuff. And though our garage sale was thrown together at the last minute, we did it up big! Even as shoppers were perusing the items up for grabs, we were restocking the shelves with more junk pulled from over-crowded closets and cupboards.

And like any good garage sale, ours had that distinct beat of banking ("*Cha-ching!* Can you believe someone would actually pay for that?"), bartering ("No, I can't go that low. But I'll make you a deal and meet you in the middle."), and begging ("It's free! Please take it. We might even pay *you* to haul it away!").

As I kept beat with the rest of the clan, I noticed another sound ringing out from time to time—the clatter of disagreement over whether something was trash or treasure.

"No, no! Not that! That's mine. I love it, and I don't want to sell it!" one person would argue.

To which the other would respond, "You'll never use it again. Get rid of it!"

Children and grown-ups alike, playing tug-of-war over things that had little value or use. As this all played out, I thought to myself, *My family is full of hoarders.* And then, as if on cue, the beat of the garage sale gave way in my ears to the hymn *I Surrender All.*

> *All to Jesus I surrender,*
> *All to Him I freely give;*
> *I will ever love and trust Him,*
> *In His presence daily live.*
> *(Refrain)*
> *I surrender all, I surrender all;*
> *All to Thee, my blessed Savior,*
> *I surrender all.*[1]

It's so easy to get swept up in the beauty of this hymn without really considering the pledge that we make to the Lord when we sing it. "I surrender all." *All.* What does that mean, all?

For me, it means that I surrendered a great job and a really big life in order to commit to four years of grueling, financially-draining seminary studies (at the age of forty, no less). It also means that I have submitted my heart-felt desire of marriage and family to the Lord, who has chosen to keep me single. It means that I have surrendered financial security to the Lord, trusting Him with the ministry call on my life that may or may not come with a paycheck. And it means that I have to lay down my longing for the independent life I once lived, at least for now. *Isn't that enough, God?* I have pondered in my heart over the past couple of days.

His response: "No. I want it *all.*"

What more do I have to give to You? my heart asks.

His answer: "Let's start with the *fear* you are harboring in your heart. And how about that *bitterness* and *resentment* you are tight-fisting? I do believe there is some *unforgiveness* that needs to be cleaned out. And while we're at it, I want your *anger,* your *envy,* your *hate,* your *pride,* your *self-righteousness,* and, last but certainly not least, your *unbelief.*"

You would think I would have jumped into action, clearing away all of that trash. Instead, my response was, "No, no! Not that! I can't give you *that!*"

It sounds strange, but parting with all of that garbage is scarier to me than parting with everything else I have already surrendered. The world's "trash" has become my "treasure." I am a spiritual hoarder, afraid to release things that are of no use to me in my walk with and service to the Lord.

What about you? If God planted a garage sale sign in your heart, are there things you are afraid to surrender? What do you look at and say, "No, no! Not that!"?

The truth is, Jesus has already paid the price for all the junk we hoard in our hearts. And He didn't barter, bargain, or nickel-and-dime us for it. He paid the highest price that anyone has ever paid or ever will pay for a bunch of trash. He settled our sin debt on the Cross with the currency of His own blood.

So how do we give up the tug-of-war with God and surrender all? A good place to start is in the Letter to the Philippians, where Paul leads us down the path of purging all the stuff in our lives that has no spiritual value.

First, Paul considers the things that this world tells us to treasure—things like relentless, self-focused ambition; self-made success; righteous anger; and membership among the elite. The apostle doesn't mince any words when he calls those worldly pursuits σκύβαλα (*skubala*), which is the ancient Greek slang word for "human excrement" (use your imagination).

> More than that, I now regard all things as liabilities compared to the far greater value of knowing Christ Jesus my Lord, for whom I have suffered the loss of all things—indeed, I regard them as dung! [*skubala*]—that I may gain Christ. (Philippians 3:8 NET)

Second, Paul says give it to God. Our hearts belong to Him anyway. Ask Him to help clear the clutter.

> Do not be anxious about anything. Instead, in every situation, through prayer and petition with thanksgiving, tell your requests to God. And the peace of God that surpasses all understanding will guard your hearts and minds in Christ Jesus. (Philippians 4:6–7 NET)

Third, Paul instructs us to focus on the things that God values, rather than what the world treasures.

Finally, brothers and sisters, whatever is true, whatever is worthy of respect, whatever is just, whatever is pure, whatever is lovely, whatever is commendable, if something is excellent or praiseworthy, think about these things. (Philippians 4:8 NET)

After a garage sale, when the clutter is cleared, we see the beauty of space. There's room to display and enjoy things that are really worth keeping. The same can be said for our hearts. God doesn't want to take all of that stuff out just to leave our hearts empty. On the contrary, He wants us to surrender to Him all of that trash that we treasure so He can make our hearts and our lives full in Him.

Lord,
I admit that I am a spiritual hoarder.
Where my heart should be filled with love,
forgiveness, and pure adoration for You,
it is bursting at the seams
with pride, unforgiveness, disobedience, and fear.
I am afraid to surrender my heart-garbage to You,
because it seems easier to live with it than without it.
That's a lie straight out of the pit of hell. I know.
Lord, forgive me for placing more value
on the clutter in my heart than on You.
I can live without all of that garbage.
But I can't live without You.
Help me make room in my heart only for You
and that which honors and glorifies You.
In the freeing Name of Jesus Christ,
and for His glory and honor.
Amen.

The Last Ship

One of my favorite summer pastimes is to stumble across a fresh, new TV series that stirs the stagnant summertime airwaves. In 2014, I climbed aboard TNT's *The Last Ship* and became immersed in my favorite summer series of all time. *The Last Ship* is a post-apocalyptic drama in which a global pandemic has wiped out the majority of the world's population. But one US naval vessel—the USS *Nathan James*—was out to sea as the fast-spreading virus ravaged the world's population. Uninfected, the brave sailors set course to save the human race.

One episode in that first season was especially intriguing to me. The weary and dehydrated crew of the *Nathan James* came to the end of freshwater, and worse, themselves. Afloat in a lame ship on a vast sea of salt water, they were weary, dangerously dehydrated, and all out of human ingenuity to survive.

So what did they do? Brace yourself. They turned to God! One of the crewmembers opened his Bible and began reading the words of Moses to the Israelites as they stood trapped between an advancing Egyptian army and the vast Red Sea wishing that they had never made the journey out of Egypt in the first place:

> Moses answered the people, "Do not be afraid. Stand firm and you will see the deliverance the LORD will bring you today. ... The LORD will fight for you; you need only to be still." (Exodus 14:13–14 NIV)

I hate that I was so surprised by this scene. But sadly, pop culture has succeeded in removing God from most storylines, replacing divinity with idolatry, vanity, and moral poverty. Seeing the crew of *The Last Ship* turn to God and His Word was as refreshing to me as the drinkable water they found at the end of the episode.

Immediately after they prayed, a strong wind suddenly filled the ship's massive sails (that they had "MacGyvered" out of parachutes), and the *Nathan James* made it safely to nearby land and potable water. The crew lived to sail another day and bring mankind back from the brink of extinction. *Whew!*

Coincidentally, that same summer the highly contagious and deadly Ebola virus presented a real-life, global threat. The images that came back from Liberia, the "hot zone," were incomprehensible. Doctors and nurses, covered from head to toe in protective gear that looked more fitting for a trip to the moon, risked their lives to help the tortured victims of this hideous disease. A childhood friend of mine was among those brave aid workers. With no cure to offer, all she could do most of the time was put her gloved hand in the hand of a dying patient and tell them how much God loved them. No words can describe the horror and hope that co-mingled with the contagion that killed thousands.

As hospitals in the US went on high alert for Ebola, I wondered if *The Last Ship* could be art imitating life. The notion that convulses with daily chaos and heaves with fear isn't that far-fetched in today's world. The poison that infected Adam and Eve with disobedience runs through the veins of every man, woman, and child on the planet—giving rise to terrorism, war, cancer, idolatry, immorality, child abuse, the corruption of marriage and family, and all other evils, including Ebola.

I am from a generation that came of age in the scary shadow of nuclear war. When the very real fear of an Ebola pandemic rose around the world, that familiar sense of impending doom from my childhood returned. What if my friend in Liberia is infected with this hideous disease? What if a few contagious travelers make it past checkpoints and expose people in this country? I used to live within walking distance of the Dallas hospital that was exposed to a man dying from Ebola. What if my *neighbors* are in danger? *Could I be in danger?* Suddenly, a disease that I had never heard of had seized my heart, mind, and even my prayers with terror. God let me stew on it for a while.

And then, He gently reminded me that even if Ebola is the thing that brings humanity to the edge of extinction, there is nothing to fear. He always has and always will be the Captain of this ship. And its course was set before He spoke this world into existence.

> You will be hearing of wars and rumors of wars. See that you are not frightened, for those things must take place, but that is not yet the end. For nation will rise against nation, and kingdom against kingdom, and in various places there will be famines and earthquakes. But all these things are merely the beginning of birth pangs. (Matthew 24:6–8)

Terror, tragedy, disease, and death should not cause us to fear—they should cause us to persevere. We can't see how it will all turn out. *But He can.* He wrote the story! And inside sources tell us we are going to love the finale.

> Whenever a woman is in labor she has pain, because her hour has come; but when she gives birth to the child, she no longer remembers the anguish because of the joy that a child has been born into the world. Therefore you too have grief now; but I will see you again, and your heart will rejoice, and no one will take your joy away from you. (John 16:21–22)

I doubt the producers of *The Last Ship* intended to buoy their summer series with deep biblical truth about our faithful, promise-keeping God. But I love how the Lord can use anything—even a summertime TV drama—to remind me of who He is. He is the Creator God of the Universe who gives weight to the wind and determines where salt water ends and fresh water begins (Job 28:25).

> The LORD is my light and my salvation.
> Whom shall I fear?
> The LORD is the defense of my life.
> Whom shall I dread? (Psalm 27:1)

Sovereign and Holy God,
In a world that oozes from the open wounds of war, terrorism,
illness, injustice, family strife, immorality, and idolatry,
it seems impossible to not be afraid.
Yet, Your Word says that we have nothing to fear
if we have put our trust in You.
In fact, fear signals that we do not completely trust You.
I can wrap my brain around that truth,
but I haven't been able to wrap my heart around it.
Help me to do that, Lord,
to trust in You with all my heart,
for my sake and Your glory.
Amen.

In Times of Terror, How Do We Pray?

I have lost count of the times over the past couple of years that I have dropped to my knees in anguish and sorrow for victims of terror. Nice, France—eighty-four innocents slaughtered at a Bastille Day celebration. Brussels—thirty-four travelers massacred in the airport and subway. Paris—130 soccer fans and party-goers brutally murdered. Orlando—nearly fifty gunned down in a nightclub. Syria—countless numbers of men, women, and children butchered.

While most of the victims are unknown to us, the horrific experience of terrorism is not. We look into the eyes of survivors and mourners and see the frightening reflection of 9/11 staring back at us. We remember what it felt like on September 11, 2001, when our own country was rocked to its core by evil incarnate.

Following the Paris attacks in November 2015, the savages who claimed responsibility for the carnage warned that their appetite for blood had only increased: "The American blood is best and we will taste it soon" was repeated over and over on jihadist websites.[2] Chilling, because we know they mean it.

So please know that what I am about to ask you to consider comes from a conflicted heart. I, too, want these rabid animals to pay for the innocent blood they have shed and continue to shed worldwide. They are evil and wicked and must be stopped! But while world leaders strategize over military tactics to defeat ISIS and other extremists, what if we, as Christ-followers, prayed for our vicious persecutors?

I know, I know. I don't like asking that question as much as you don't like hearing it. But stay with me for a minute, please.

For months now, the Lord has prompted me to pray for His supernatural strength to fortify Christians facing deadly persecution throughout the world. The Spirit has led me to regularly lift up fellow believers who stand at the tip of the spear: *Lord, please give Your strength to those who are facing death because of their love for You. Help them to stand firmly in their faith, no matter their circumstances. Be merciful and deliver them quickly—one way or another—and reward them for their faithfulness.*

Then not too long ago, the Lord added a rather shocking twist to that petition. *Father, make Your witness so strong that it stops even the most heinous of persecutors dead in his tracks, long enough to at least consider the hope found in Your Son—the hope he sees in the eyes of his victims.*

Trust me, that is not an easy prayer to offer. But I've heard about a man who admitted to finding great purpose in hunting Christians. He was merciless in his mission to make Christ-followers pay for their faith. One day he was stopped dead in his tracks by the Lord who blindsided him with the Truth of the Gospel. Every day since, this man has testified to the life-saving, life-transforming power of Christ. And countless people have been saved after hearing his story.

What's this man's name? *Paul.* We find his story in the Book of Acts. And we can learn a lot from him about being a Christ-follower by reading his Letter to the Romans, as well as his Letters to the Corinthians, Galatians, Ephesians, Colossians, Thessalonians, Timothy, Titus, and Philemon. Paul is one of our spiritual heroes.

But when we first meet him in Scripture, he is an up-and-coming member of the Jewish elite. Well-educated, wealthy, influential, highly-respected, and dangerously zealous, Paul (or Saul as he was first known by the Jews) was as loyal as they come to the rabid ideology behind the murder of Jesus and the subsequent persecution of all Christ-followers, including Stephen. As it turns out, Saul held the robes of the men who stoned Stephen. He was there when Stephen voiced his final request on earth.

> Then falling on his knees, he cried out with a loud voice, "Lord, do not hold this sin against them!" Having said this, he fell asleep. (Acts 7:60)

Wow! Talk about loving your enemy! But was Saul transformed by Stephen's prayer? No! He actually seemed to be fueled by the barbaric execution of Stephen. This first century jihadist immediately set out on his mission to "ravage" the church (Acts 8:1–3).

But not long after that (some scholars argue it was a matter of months), the young, bloodthirsty zealot met the Risen Christ on the road to Damascus, and his life was forever transformed (Acts 9:1–31).

> As he was traveling, it happened that he was approaching Damascus, and suddenly a light from heaven flashed around him; and he fell to the ground and heard a voice saying to him, "Saul, Saul, why are you persecuting Me?" And he said, "Who are You, Lord?" And He said, "I am Jesus whom you are persecuting, but get up and enter the city, and it will be told you what you must do." (Acts 9:3–6)

> Now for several days he was with the disciples who were at Damascus, and immediately he began to proclaim Jesus in the synagogues, saying, "He is the Son of God." All those hearing him continued to be amazed, and were saying, "Is this not he who in Jerusalem destroyed those who called on this name, and who had come here for the purpose of bringing them bound before the chief priests?" But Saul kept increasing in strength and confounding the Jews who lived at Damascus by proving that this Jesus is the Christ. (Act 9:19–22)

Think about it. God took a man as vicious as any ISIS terrorist and turned him into a fierce warrior for Christ, who we now know as the apostle Paul—the man who, under the inspiration of the Holy Spirit, wrote most of the New Testament!

If God can transform the hate-filled heart of Saul, can He not do the same for modern-day persecutors? Just a few months ago, a one-time ISIS jihadist admitted to Youth With A Mission (YWAM) missionaries that he killed Christians and enjoyed it. But there came a time during his deadly rampage when he began to dream about Jesus. And then one of his victims gave the man his Bible. As the story is reported by YWAM, the ISIS fighter still killed the Christian man. But he took the Bible and read it. Today, that former ISIS jihadist is living his life for Christ.

So what do you think? Do we dare add to our prayers the evil men who have committed unspeakable atrocities in the name of their god? Admittedly, I bristle at the notion. But, ultimately, I say yes. For the glory of God—yes! Paul is a real-life example of what our God—the One True God—can and will do with a bloodthirsty maniac. Imagine the impact a terrorist-turned-Christ-follower can have on this world that desperately needs hope!

Heavenly Father,
You are holy and just, and You promise
that the wicked will pay for their evil deeds.
But You also promise that the one who turns to You,
no matter what he has done, will be forgiven.
That's hard to swallow sometimes,
that the one who is gleefully spilling the blood
of Your people today could be covered in the atoning blood
of Christ tomorrow.
The apostle Paul shows us that even the darkest of hearts
cannot overcome the light of Christ.
So, Lord, if it is Your will, let it be so.
From the kingdom of darkness,
raise up mighty warriors for Your Kingdom.
And please, Lord,
give strength and courage to Your people
who are suffering for Your Name's sake.
In Christ's Name and for His glory and honor.
Amen.

CHAPTER 3

Basement
Reflections
on
Uncertainty

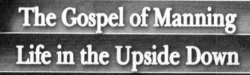

The Gospel of Manning

It was a bittersweet thing, seeing Peyton Manning retire from football after leading my beloved Denver Broncos to victory in Super Bowl 50. What fun it was watching #18 master his craft and manhandle some of the toughest NFL players and teams on the planet. But "The Sheriff" won't be back in town to lead the Broncos to another Super Bowl victory. Peyton Manning is undeniably one of football's all-time greats, and we will miss him. It is a bitter pill to swallow.

But, oh, how sweet it was to hear the hope that he still has for a purposeful and productive future. As Peyton expressed in his retirement speech, "I'm totally convinced that the end of my football career is just the beginning of something I haven't even discovered yet. Life is not shrinking for me. It's morphing into a whole new world of possibilities."[1]

When I heard him say goodbye with such confidence and optimism, two of my greatest passions—God's Word and football (especially the Broncos)—collided on the gridiron of life. I don't want to over-spiritualize the words of Peyton Manning. He's The Sheriff, not the Messiah. But his attitude of staying hopeful and curious about an unknown future got me thinking about Jesus' disciples when they faced extreme uncertainty in the hours and days after His death.

Prior to His crucifixion, Jesus tried to prepare His followers for those dark days.

From that time Jesus began to show His disciples that He must go to Jerusalem, and suffer many things from the elders and chief

41

priests and scribes, and be killed, and be raised up on the third day. (Matthew 16:21)

He tried to get them to understand that His life on earth had to end so that the next season of their lives as Kingdom-builders could begin.

But I tell you the truth, it is to your advantage that I go away; for if I do not go away, the Helper will not come to you; but if I go, I will send Him to you. (John 16:7)

But they simply could not wrap their brains and hearts around His death. The man they believed was the long-awaited Messiah—the conquering King who would free them from the oppression of their enemies—died. *Died!* It was all for nothing. They had given up everything—family, homes, livelihoods, and security—to follow Jesus. When He breathed His last on that cross, their hopes and dreams perished with Him. Listen in as two Christ-followers traveled back home from Jerusalem in utter discouragement and disappointment.

And they were talking with each other about all these things which had taken place. While they were talking and discussing, Jesus Himself approached and began traveling with them. But their eyes were prevented from recognizing Him. And He said to them, "What are these words that you are exchanging with one another as you are walking?" And they stood still, looking sad. One of them, named Cleopas, answered and said to Him, "Are You the only one visiting Jerusalem and unaware of the things which have happened here in these days?" And He said to them, "What things?" And they said to Him, "The things about Jesus the Nazarene, who was a prophet mighty in deed and word in the sight of God and all the people, and how the chief priests and our rulers delivered Him to the sentence of death, and crucified Him. But we were hoping that it was He who was going to redeem Israel. (Luke 24:14–21)

"But we were hoping …" When the life they had envisioned with Jesus looked far different than their reality, they threw in the towel. Everything that had given their lives meaning and value was gone, or so they thought.

And He said to them, "O foolish men and slow of heart to believe in all that the prophets have spoken! Was it not necessary for the Christ to suffer these things and to enter into His glory?" Then beginning with Moses and with all the prophets, He explained to them the things concerning Himself in all the Scriptures. (Luke 24:25–27)

Discouragement and fear of an unknown future had gotten the best of them, so much so that they didn't recognize their Teacher, even as He guided them through all of the prophesies, events, and promises that pointed toward His incarnation.

During times of uncertainty I have also traveled that path of unbelief. Have you? What we learn on the road to Emmaus is that even during times of darkness, when we can barely see in front of our noses, we can be assured that our future as Christ-followers has never looked brighter, because it is in His hands.

"Football has taught me not to be led by obstructions and setbacks, but instead to be led by dreams,"[2] The Sheriff said before riding off into the sunset. Let Manning's final play call be an encouragement to all of us.

If God has given us the breath of life, He has given us purpose in life. It may be difficult to see that purpose in the midst of uncertainty. But remaining curious and optimistic as we wait on Him enables us to embrace the unknown seasons to come.

Happy trails, Peyton!

Father God,
Thank You that You enter into our everyday lives
and passions (even football) to reveal Your character to us.
Just like the disciples on the road to Emmaus,
I can be so blinded by the uncertainty of life that
I lose sight of Your faithfulness.
You, and You alone, will never let me down.
By Your Spirit,
help me to remember that when I get lost
in seasons of darkness, confusion, and uncertainty.
Amen.

Life in the Upside Down

A friend recently described how he feels living in this world that seems to have become completely unhinged. "It's as if you're holding a cup of coffee, but everyone around you says it's lemonade, and pretty soon you start wondering if it really is lemonade!"

Right is wrong and wrong is right. Truth is relative. The guys in our society who used to wear the black hats are now being publicly crowned with white hats, while the real white-hat guys are being picked off, one by one. And to add to the lunacy and uncertainty of today's world, there is mass confusion over which bathroom to use! I don't know about you, but there are days (way too many of late) when I just can't get my bearings. It feels like the world is completely upside down.

"The world *is* upside down," a steadying voice whispers to my heart.

God created man in His own image, in the image of God He created him; male and female He created them. God blessed them; and God said to them, "Be fruitful and multiply, and fill the earth, and subdue it; and rule over the fish of the sea and over the birds of the sky and over every living thing that moves on the earth." (Genesis 1:27–28)

Once upon a time, all was right and well with the world. The Creator looked out on His Creation and declared that it was "very good" (Genesis 1:31). Divine order ruled supreme, and chaos had no place in the world.

Then, one day, everything got upended!

> Now the serpent was more crafty than any beast of the field which the LORD God had made. And he said to the woman, "Indeed, has God said, 'You shall not eat from any tree of the garden'?" The woman said to the serpent, "From the fruit of the trees of the garden we may eat." (Genesis 3:1–2)

Stop right there. Do you see it? The woman *responded* to the Serpent. She had God-given dominion over this "living thing that moves on the earth." And yet, she gives him her ear, and, ultimately, she and the man surrender their authority to the beast. *That* is the moment God's natural order of the universe was turned on its head. And it has been upside down and right-side-wrong ever since.

Lord, chaos seems to be gaining traction! We're losing ground as each new day brings headlines of just how twisted and savage man can be. What are we going to do? What can I do?! I cry out to the Lord.

"Do your job," He firmly responds in the recesses of my heart. "Yes, my daughter, the world is experiencing crazy times. But what has changed for you?"

Nothing, I quickly realize. Except that now more than ever I need to do what He has called me to do. As the apostle Paul put it, "To live is Christ" (Philippians 1:21).

I am reminded that I exist to honor and glorify the Lord. My chief purpose on earth is to tell hurting people about a loving God who endured unimaginable insanity for us. Think about it. Creation tried to kill its Creator! Now that's messed up. Madness magnified to the Nth degree! And our Savior, Jesus Christ, voluntarily entered into it so that we—you and I—would one day have a way out of it and into His eternal presence.

Here's the deal friends. Things are probably going to get a whole lot worse before they get better (I'm not a pessimist. I've just read the end of the Book). Without a crystal ball, life is uncertain. And every new day in this upside down world will likely deliver more sorrow, loss, suffering, and chaos. But it also delivers more opportunity to give increasing numbers of hurting people hope, the kind of hope that can't be won in an election, lost in battle, or stolen by blood-thirsty thugs.

God has given me new perspective on living upside down. As it turns out, it's the perfect vantage point for seeing His purpose with my life. How about you? Can you see your God-given purpose in the upside down?

Merciful and loving God,
Thank You that You still love Your Creation,
even though Your Creation has turned on You.
I cannot imagine the heartbreak You endure
when the very thing You deemed "good" is turned upside down
by a crafty enemy who seeks to kill and destroy.
Lord, no matter how confusing and uncertain
life gets in this insane world,
steady me with Your presence;
strengthen me with Your Truth;
surround me with people
who love You and seek Your face;
and satisfy me the love, hope, and peace
that only You can provide.
I worship You and offer these requests
in the powerful Name of Christ.
To Him be the glory forever and ever.
Amen.

Who Can Sleep at a Time Like This?

Have you ever felt like you are on a sinking ship in this world? Life as a Christ-follower seems to get more distressing and uncertain by the day as story after story of Christian persecution surfaces (not just in the Middle East, but in America and worldwide). And yet, rarely do we see an influential Christian or political leader take a public stand against the global assault on our faith.

Hello! Who's steering the ship here? We're taking on water fast! DO SOMETHING!

> And there arose a fierce gale of wind, and the waves were breaking over the boat so much that the boat was already filling up. Jesus Himself was in the stern, asleep on the cushion; and they woke Him and said to Him, "Teacher, do You not care that we are perishing?" And He got up and rebuked the wind and said to the sea, "Hush, be still." And the wind died down and it became perfectly calm. And He said to them, "Why are you afraid? Do you still have no faith?" (Mark 4:37–40)

Three of the four Gospels record this violent event on the Sea of Galilee—a very real crisis that scared the living daylights out of Jesus' disciples! On this side of the Cross, we can look down our noses at them and say, "Seriously, guys! You're in the boat with God, the Creator and Master of storms. Chill out!" But the disciples didn't have the benefit of hindsight. All they could see was the water lapping over the sides of their vessel threatening to either throw them overboard or splinter apart and sink underneath them. Any security they felt with Christ was blurred by the wind and waves that assaulted their faith.

In the Greek, Mark and Luke use λαῖλαψ (*lailaps*) to describe the storm as a "hurricane" or a "whirlwind," referring to the wild gales that tossed the boat about. For modern-day perspective, think about Hurricane Katrina that slammed into the Gulf Coast with 175 mph winds (2005). Or consider the catastrophic tornado in Joplin, Missouri, that literally twisted the life out of a large portion of that little community (2011).

Matthew points to a different but equally terrifying element of the storm—the violent shaking caused by the waters heaving underneath the boat. It was like an underwater earthquake. Interestingly, Matthew uses the exact same word to describe the convulsion that occurred when the stone was rolled away from Christ's tomb (Matthew 27:54). Are you starting to get the picture of what was going on out there in the middle of the Galilee? These guys weren't sissies. They were experienced fishermen who had weathered a storm or two. But this wasn't just *any* storm. It was an *epic* tempest—supernaturally fierce!

And Jesus slept through it.

"Save us, Lord; we are *perishing!*" shouted the terrified disciples as they rousted their Master from His slumber. (Matthew 8:25, emphasis mine)

Their Master responded, first to the wind and waves. "Hush, be still" (Mark 4:39). Then, when all was perfectly still, Jesus turned to His disciples, "Why are you afraid? Do you still have no faith?" (Mark 4:40).

Jesus' reaction has always confused me. It seems a bit harsh given that the disciples were caught off guard by this ferocious storm. Rather than considering Jesus' response in its entirety, I have made the mistake of focusing only on His question: "Do you still have no faith?"

Look back at what Jesus did before He addressed His disciples. He admonished the storm. "Hush, be still." With three words, Jesus silenced the winds and settled the waves.

Jesus wasn't convicting the disciples of their fear. He was calling them to faith—faith in Him, as the Sovereign Authority over all of creation, including the elements of nature which He can control with a single word. "Hush!"

When that Truth really sinks into the heart of a Christ-follower, there is nothing in this world that can sink one's faith. Never has this been more evident to me than in the life of Dr. J. Dwight Pentecost ("Dr. P"), who entered into the presence of the Lord on April 28, 2014, at the age of ninety-nine years and four days. Several months before he died, I asked Dr. P how he reacted when he first received his cancer diagnosis. I can still hear the tones of certainty and security that accompanied his response: "Well, when you live with someone as long as I have, you just know them. I know I can trust Him."

Dr. Pentecost lived with Jesus on earth for nearly a century. This man of God fell deeply in love with the Lord and His Word in the midst of some very dark and uncertain days for his country and his family, including two World Wars, the Great Depression, 9/11, the loss of his wife, and the unexpected death of a daughter. But life didn't capsize Dr. Pentecost's faith. Life shaped his faith as he learned to trust the Master in *all* circumstances.

Yes, these are stormy and uncertain times for Christians, and if you've read the end of the Book, you know it's only going to get more turbulent from here. But fear not, Christ-follower. In the wind, we find strength, and on the waves, we gain our balance. And at just the right time, the One who spoke the wind and the water into existence will say, "Hush!" And there will be *peace*.

Sovereign Lord and Master,
I don't know for sure how I would have responded
had I been in that boat on Galilee.
But it is likely that I would have been screaming
louder than anyone else.
How many times have You called me to faith
and I have responded with fear?
I have focused on the power of the storms,
rather than trusting in the One
who has power over the storms.
Lord, help me to wrap my brain and my heart
and my life around Your Sovereignty.

Through the power of Your Word and Spirit,
enable me to know You so well
that nothing can rock my world,
and when I put my head down at night,
I can sleep—in peace.
I offer this prayer in the matchless
Name of my all-powerful Savior,
Jesus Christ, the Prince of Peace.
Amen.

Swimming in Quicksand

Just when you think our world can't get any more absurd and depraved, another secret e-mail reveals corruption in the highest ranks of government, another accusation of sexual maleficence is leveled, another natural disaster pounds an already broken and battered country, and another group of faithful Christ-followers are driven from their homes, some to their graves.

And that's only the background noise to the cacophony of your personal life that rises and falls on faith and fear, loyalty and betrayal, blessing and loss, good health and disease. All the madness and uncertainty in the world seems to magnify the crazy in our own lives, and I will admit that there are days when I just want to throw in the towel.

On one of those days recently, a friend made a simple but profound statement that has become my battle cry. "The only way you get to know the end of your story is if you don't quit."

Who doesn't love a great story? And as Christ-followers, we can be confident that our life-stories will have an awesome ending.

> We know that God causes all things to work together for good to those who love God, to those who are called according to His purpose. (Romans 8:28)

But when the plot of life thickens, it can feel like quicksand swallowing us into a hopeless quagmire. *Seriously God? This is not how I would have written my memoirs,* I have often lamented. Have you ever said, or at least thought, that? I'm guessing most of God's people down through the ages have questioned the Lord's presence and purpose in the hard chapters of life when the future seems so uncertain. Fortunately, God shares with us the life-stories of a few saints who never gave up and lived to tell others about His faithfulness. Joseph is one of my favorites.

As a young man, his own brothers sold him into slavery. But Joseph didn't lie down and die. He figured out not only how to survive, but how to thrive as a slave. Just when things started to go his way, he was falsely accused of sexual assault and thrown into prison. Left to rot in a dungeon, Joseph had every reason to wave the white flag. Instead, he took the time behind bars to practice his God-given gift of discernment, which ultimately earned him his freedom and the keys to a kingdom that would save God's people from starvation. At every twist and turn in the plot line of Joseph's life (Genesis 37–50), Scripture tells us that God was with him, *enabling* him to swim in the quicksand. And in the final chapter of Joseph's life, his story comes full circle as he shares with his brothers what he learned about the Lord in the darkest of days.

> Then his brothers also came and fell down before him and said, "Behold, we are your servants." But Joseph said to them, "Do not be afraid, for am I in God's place? As for you, you meant evil against me, but God meant it for good in order to bring about this present result, to preserve many people alive. (Genesis 50:18–20)

Under the weight of your own burdens, you might argue that Joseph was a super saint, a man with supernatural powers who was destined for greatness. Guess what? *So are you!*

> But if the Spirit of Him who raised Jesus from the dead dwells in you, He who raised Christ Jesus from the dead will also give life to your mortal bodies through His Spirit who dwells in you. (Romans 8:11)

Pause for a moment and try to wrap your brain around that! The *Spirit of God* resides within you and equips you with the power of the resurrection, the power to persevere and live victoriously, even in the quicksand. Broken relationships, unemployment, financial distress, addiction, abuse, betrayal, false accusations, whatever your quicksand is, you are equipped by the Spirit to overcome it. And when you do, what a God story you will have to tell!

"The only way you get to know the end of your story is if you don't quit."

Let this be the battle cry of all Christ-followers in these uncertain times. Things may seem bleak and almost hopelessness now. But our story isn't over, dear friends. And as one who has read the Book from start to finish, I can confidently say it has the greatest ending of all time!

Father God,
You are the greatest storyteller of all time and
I am so grateful that You have included me
in Your storyline.
But as it is with any good book,
especially Your Good Book,
there are unexpected twists and turns.
Lord, thank You that You promise to help me
navigate this life on earth from the first page to the last.
And, oh, how blessed I am to know that
when my life story on earth ends,
the sequel picks up in Heaven.
By Your Spirit, help me to embrace the story
You have written for me—even the seasons
when it feels like I'm sinking in quicksand.
You and You alone can teach me to swim.
I love You, Lord.
In Christ's Name and for His glory, I pray.
Amen.

CHAPTER 4

Basement Reflections
on
Pain and Grief

Happiness Seems So Far Away

Look at Me!

Whose Right to Life?

Weep or Reap?

Happiness Seems So Far Away

"Happiness seems so far away." I have said that more times than I can count over the past few years as life has imploded around me. I have grieved my own hopes and dreams that have slipped away. I've helplessly watched loved ones endure unthinkable abuse, pain, and loss. And I've witnessed my beloved country splintering into bitter and angry factions that seem beyond repair. They all prompt the same conclusion: *Happiness seems so far away.*

But is that right thinking? Is "happiness" a destination, and if so, shouldn't a daughter of the King of the Universe be able to live there?

There is no shortage of theories on happiness. Countless authors tackle the topic with titles like *The Art of Happiness; Stumbling on Happiness; The How of Happiness; Hardwiring Happiness; The Happiness Project* (a *New York Times* Best Seller); and my favorite—*The 18 Rules Of Happiness Pocket Guide.*[1] Seriously? Eighteen rules in your pocket!

Forget trying to find truth on Amazon. I went straight to the book I trust the most—the Bible. And what I found was really quite surprising. The Greek word for *happiness* (in the sense of prosperity or good fortune) is εὐδαιμονία (*eudaimonía*). And it cannot be found anywhere in the Gospels or the Epistles. Neither Jesus nor His disciples ever used the word for "happiness" that relates to prosperity or good fortune. How can that be? After all, isn't happiness something to which we are entitled? Our own Declaration of Independence, which was penned by God-fearing men, claims it as a "right."

We hold these truths to be self-evident, that all men are created equal, that they are endowed by their Creator with certain unalienable Rights, that among these are Life, Liberty and the pursuit of Happiness.

But Jesus doesn't tell us to expect happiness. Rather, He tries to prepare His followers for a life of struggle, heartache, and suffering in this world.

Remember the word that I said to you, 'A slave is not greater than his master.' If they persecuted Me, they will also persecute you. (John 15:20)

In the world you have tribulation, but take courage; I have overcome the world. (John 16:33)

Don't get me wrong. I don't believe that God intends for us to move through our days with our heads hanging low and our knuckles dragging on the ground. He provides seasons in our lives when we can be deliriously happy—like when we fall in love; when a baby is born; when an exciting, new job comes with a bigger paycheck; when we can trade snow and ice for sand and water (I'm big on this one!); and when the doctor says the cancer is gone. "Happiness" is achievable. But it is also elusive.

For the pagans in ancient Greece, εὐδαιμονία (*eudaimonía*) was considered to be the result of being protected by a good god. Built from words *eu* ("good") and *daimōn* ("spirit"), the ancient Greek word actually aligns pretty well with the twenty-first century pop-culture definition of happiness: the good life, freedom from suffering, flourishing, well-being, joy, prosperity, pleasure.[2]

In today's world, we idolize health, wealth, and prosperity. If you have those three things, you have happiness. But just as health, wealth, and prosperity come and go, so does the elusive happiness. Even Robin Williams, a comedic genius who made the world laugh for decades, couldn't hold onto it. His battles with addiction, depression, and Parkinson's disease literally strangled the happiness out of him. Happiness seems so far away.

Before you hit the exit button out of despair, let me give you some good news—joy! In Scripture, God uses the word *joy* a lot. And He tells us that it is as close as the beat of our own hearts.

And the disciples were continually filled with joy and with the Holy Spirit. (Acts 13:52)

The Greek word for *joy*, χαρά (*chara*), is all over the New Testament. Used two dozen times in the Gospels and nearly twenty times by Paul in his letters, χαρά is often associated with a work of the Lord. For Christ-followers, joy is a product of the Holy Spirit who lives within us!

But the fruit of the Spirit is love, joy, peace, patience, kindness, goodness, faithfulness. (Galatians 5:22)

We may not be happy in our worldly circumstances, but we can have joy, because joy is a product of our relationship with the Lord, not the world.

Just hours before His crucifixion, as Jesus was praying for His disciples (including us), He said to the Father:

But now I come to You; and these things I speak in the world so that they may have My joy made full in themselves. (John 17:13)

Jesus found full and complete joy in being obedient to the Father, even to the point of death. It is obedience to God that brings true joy into our lives. Jesus mapped out the journey to joy for us.

Let us run with endurance the race that is set before us, fixing our eyes on Jesus, the author and perfecter of faith, who *for the joy set before Him* endured the cross, despising the shame, and has sat down at the right hand of the throne of God. (Hebrews 12:1–2, emphasis mine)

To experience the full measure of biblical joy—which has nothing to do with what this world has to offer—we need to fully submit to the will of the Lord. The late Dr. J. Dwight Pentecost, my beloved pastor, mentor, and truly joy-filled friend, lived by this truth: The key to joy is the centrality of Christ in our lives.

To please the Father is the dominating desire of Jesus' life, so that at the Cross He could say, "I have set the Father before me, and I press persistently, singly, unswervingly in fulfilling that which He has given to me to do." If the joy that the Lord Jesus knew came from His obedience to God, how do you think we can know the joy of God apart from the perfect obedience to His will? It is utter foolishness to think that we can find joy and contentment and satisfaction in our lives apart from perfect obedience to the Word of God and the will of God. —Dr. J. Dwight Pentecost[3]

I spent many hours with Dr. Pentecost talking about life with the Lord and what it means to be a Christ-follower. I wish that I could write to him in Heaven and tell him that I have finally found the pure joy he often spoke of. The truth is, I have put far more energy into pursuing worldly happiness (which for me is the absence of suffering) than biblical joy. But I can confidently say that joy is coming into view as I press on with the goal of making my Savior, and not my circumstances, the center of my life.

Yes. Happiness still seems so far away.

But that's okay. Joy is where I am headed anyway. Where are you headed today?

God of true joy,
While the world tries to offer happiness,
You offer something more valuable
than thousands of pieces of gold and silver: joy.
That good and satisfying thing is found through
obedience to Your Word and will for our lives.
Forgive me, Lord, for setting my sights on happiness
and losing sight of what my heart truly desires—joy.
By Your Spirit, enable me to know Your will for my life.
And with the courage and strength that can only come from You,
help me to accomplish Your will in a way
that honors and glorifies You, no matter my circumstances.
Thank You, Lord,
for giving to me good gifts that have produced happiness
including loving friends and family; meaningful work;

the opportunity to live and worship in freedom;
an abundance of food, shelter, clothing, and healthcare;
and my four-legged buddies who are always glad to see me.
I am overwhelmed by Your generosity and provision.
But even more so, I am overwhelmed by the Truth that
if any or all of these gifts were taken from me,
joy would remain.
Thank You for teaching me that Truth.
In the Name of Your Son, Jesus Christ,
who for the joy set before Him endured the Cross.
Amen.

Look at Me!

"Look at Me," I heard the Lord gently but firmly whisper to my broken heart.

On my knees, crying out to Him for the umpteenth time over the cruelties of life and people, I begged Him to make it stop. I couldn't take any more sorrow. I was tired of being mistreated. I didn't want to expose myself to any more betrayal. My heart hurt too much to quietly endure more abuse for the sake of others as I had been doing for months (make that years). *Look at me, Lord! I am at the end of my rope!*

"No. Look at Me," that still, small voice resounded in my soul. My mind's eye focused squarely on the Cross. And I wept.

When we are hurting so much that we don't think we can take another minute of this life, do we dare look past our own tears into the bloodied, swollen, weary, tortured eyes of our Lord hanging on the Cross? Do we dare to look at Him, really look at Him, and say, "Not my will but Yours, Lord. I will follow You wherever You take me"?

Contrary to biblical lore, it is unlikely that the Cross of Christ stood at a distance on a hill. Historically, the Romans used crucifixion to keep people in line. A hideous form of capital punishment that was reserved for only the worst of criminals, it prompted horror among witnesses. The intent for those terrorized by the sight was clear: *Obey* Roman rule or this is what will happen to you. And that message was intensified when a crucifixion took place roadside, at eye-level with passersby.

On Friday afternoon (especially the Friday of the annual Passover

Feast), Jerusalem streets would have been packed with people rushing about to get their errands done and get home before sundown, when the Sabbath would begin. Countless hundreds (maybe thousands) of people likely passed by the Suffering Servant, at nearly eye-level, as they hurried home to worship God.

They would have been within feet if not inches of the crucifixion. They would have seen the blood streaming down Jesus' forehead as the crown of thorns dug deeper with each of His facial contortions. And they would have smelled the sweat of anxiety and heard the heaves of Jesus and the other men subjected to slow, torturous deaths. Wads of spit would have spewed around them easily hitting their mark from just a few feet away. And that sound of tearing? It could have come from the Roman guards gathered round to rip and divide Jesus' garments, or was that a shoulder dislocating at the socket?

The contempt for Jesus Christ, Son of God, God Himself, was palpable in every way. The air was heavy with the sight, sound, and smell of a slow and barbaric murder. And yet, not one single malicious word did He utter back to the world that despised and abused Him. He quietly endured it for the sake of others, for the sake of me.

"Look at Me," that still, small voice whispers to my aching heart as the Lord focuses His brutalized, compassionate, loving eyes on mine. I have two choices: Look at Him and press into His will for my life. Or look away and press into my will, throwing my contempt back in the faces of those who have hurt me.

With that, I have a good cry, get off of my knees, and get focused on Him. He never promised that it would be easy. In fact, He warned that it would be really hard for those who follow Him. But whatever path of suffering lies ahead of us, He has already been there. There is nothing in this world that Jesus—"a man of sorrows and acquainted with grief" (Isaiah 53:3)—has not experienced and overcome. Betrayal, abuse, grief, loss, sorrow, injustice, disgrace, contempt, persecution, abandonment, you name it, He's experienced it. And He has already claimed the victory for us over it!

> "These things I have spoken to you, so that in Me you may have peace. In the world you have tribulation, but take courage; I have overcome the world." (John 16:33)

Our God who conquered death will faithfully see us through any and all of the world's assaults. So whose eyes will capture your attention and focus today? Those of the world that have contempt for you? Or those of Heaven that have conquered death for you?

The LORD bless you, and keep you;
The LORD make His face shine on you,
And be gracious to you;
The LORD lift up His countenance on you,
And give you peace. (Numbers 6:24–26)

> *Oh Lord,*
> *It is unimaginable that the Creator of the Universe*
> *would willingly submit Himself to the most heinous*
> *kind of death that man can devise.*
> *And yet You did it, for my sake.*
> *I wonder, had I been there as Your lungs heaved*
> *and Your blood co-mingled with the sweat of agony,*
> *would I have looked You in the eyes?*
> *Could I have looked You in the eyes?*
> *Lord, I want to see this world and my life*
> *circumstances through Your eyes.*
> *I want to look at my pain and grief and see victory,*
> *not the kind of victory that brings a crowd*
> *to its feet after a winning score,*
> *but the kind of victory that brings Your daughter*
> *to her knees after she realizes that her pain has purpose*
> *and that You will never leave or forsake her.*
> *When I am overcome by pain and sorrow,*
> *help me to look beyond the tears into the eyes*
> *of my Savior and say thank You.*
> *In the victorious Name of the Risen Christ.*
> *Amen.*

Whose Right to Life?

My heart sank as I learned that twenty-nine-year-old Brittany Maynard, a vibrant, adventurous newlywed chose to take her own life before cancer overtook her body.

"The day is my choice," Ms. Maynard publicly proclaimed[4] as she determined in advance that November 2, 2014, would be her last day on earth. And on that day, ten months after being diagnosed with terminal brain cancer, and less than two weeks after finishing her "bucket list" with a visit to the Grand Canyon, the young woman swallowed a lethal dose of legally prescribed medication as her family looked on.

In a highly-publicized "Death with Dignity" campaign to advance the dialogue on physician-assisted suicide, Brittany Maynard boldly asserted her "right" to live or die, saying, "I made my decisions based on my wishes, clinical research, choices, discussions with physicians, and logic. ... I have been in charge of this choice, gaining control of a terrifying terminal disease through the application of my own humane logic."[5]

I want to be clear that I am not passing judgment on Brittany Maynard. As Christ-followers, we leave that to the Lord. Our job in this world is to grieve with and pray for her family and loved ones and compassionately speak God's Truth into a world that holds a low view of life and a high view of death.

I also want to be honest and say that I am intimate with the desire to escape the pain of this world. Over the past few years, there have been nights when pain, grief, and loss seemed more than I could bear. On my knees, I have asked the Lord, *Please, God, just don't let me wake up.* A raw admission that I share only to bring a different voice to the "Death with Dignity" dialogue. I always followed up my prayer with, *If You choose to give me breath of life in the morning, Lord, I know it is because You still have purpose for me in this world.* Every day since, He has given me breath of life and the strength to endure. The Lord, my Creator, is the only one who has the "right" to my life.

The thief comes only to steal and kill and destroy. (John 10:10)

These words from the Savior, Jesus Christ, have sounded through my head and heart as I have grieved for Ms. Maynard and this worldly notion that our lives are our own and death takes more courage than life. That's a lie straight from the pit of hell. In the parable of the Good Shepherd (John 10:1–10), Jesus, the Shepherd, views man as His greatest, most treasured possession, comparing us to sheep. This metaphor would have resonated powerfully with Jesus' first century listeners who highly valued sheep for provision, commerce, and religious sacrifices. The thief, Satan (or his earthly henchmen), will do whatever it takes to find a way into the fold to steal from God's flock.

Jesus warns, "The thief comes only to steal and kill and destroy."

Steal. First, Jesus says the thief, Satan, comes to *steal.* In the Greek, this verb, κλέπτω (*kléptō*), means far more than to swipe a pack of gum from a convenience store. It is the same word used in the Ten Commandments ("Thou shalt not steal"), carrying with it a nuance of rebellion against God. The thief is not the rightful owner of the flock, but that doesn't stop him from scheming to steal that which belongs to God.

Deception of man: "It's an individual's choice whether to live or die."
Truth of God: Man doesn't choose to die. Satan swindles man out of the opportunity to live. God is in charge and died a humiliating death so that man could live!

Kill. Jesus adds that once Satan has stolen the sheep, he *kills* it. He has no desire to care for it and provide for its needs. Satan's only motive is to usurp the authority of God. Out of arrogance and defiance, he butchers God's Creation. The Greek verb *to kill* in this passage, θύω (*thuó*), means "to slaughter an animal in a ritualistic way," as a sacrifice to a deity. With the blood of the sheep, Satan serves his own twisted, voracious need for worship when worship rightfully belongs to God and God alone.

Deception of man: "I am taking control of a terrifying disease."
Truth of God: The Lord is sovereign and in control. He is the One who heals. The thief arrogantly places man on his altar as an offering for his own glory. Satan slaughters ultimate healing.

Destroy. Finally, Jesus says the thief destroys the sheep. He's already slaughtered the creature, so what more can he do? The Greek verb that Jesus uses for destroy, ἀπόλλυμι (*apollumi*), is a theological term meaning "perish" that carries with it the implication of separation from God and His people.

Deception of man: "An individual's choice of death is humane and logical."
Truth of God: Jesus Christ, Son of God, God Himself, died on the Cross and rose from the grave so man could live with Him forever. Satan convinces man to think logically rather than theologically. Hope for eternal life with the Lord perishes in the hands of the thief.

From her obituary, we read that Brittany Maynard "wanted to express a note of deep thanks to all her beautiful, smart, wonderful, supportive friends whom she 'sought out like water' during her life and illness for insight, support, and the shared experience of a beautiful life."[6]

If only it had been Living Water that she sought. What an impact this passionate, bright, beautiful young woman could have made in a world gone mad with the notion that death by suicide is more courageous than life with God.

Steal. Kill. Destroy.

Brittany Maynard's parting words to the world were: "It is people who pause to appreciate life and give thanks who are happiest. If we change our thoughts, we change our world!"[7] If she only knew how right she was.

Lord,
You are the Giver and Keeper of Life.
But from the minute I entered this world,

the Enemy has sought to convince me
that my life is in my hands, not Yours.
In seasons of suffering, I am most vulnerable to that lie.
Desperate for relief from the pain,
I want to find the easiest and fastest way out.
O Lord, how grateful I am that Your truth rises above the lie.
Your Word tells me that
You knit me together in my mother's womb.
Why would I want to unravel the work of the Master?
You sent Your Son to die for me.
Should I not be willing to live for You?
Father, I grieve for those who have been deceived
into thinking that a life with pain is a life without purpose.
When I look at the Cross,
I know that nothing could be further from the truth.
Thank You, Lord, for giving me life,
and giving me life eternal.
In the Name of Christ, my Savior.
Amen.

Weep or Reap?

Over the past few years, national events like homegrown terror attacks, political divisiveness, and Supreme Court rulings have set America on what seems to be a downward spiral. It may be impossible to fully recover the prosperity and unity that our nation once enjoyed.

In the midst of one especially distressing event, my cell phone nearly exploded with texts from friends and family who shared my sense of doom and were seeking some sort of spiritual solace. On my knees, I cried out to the Lord, *Seriously, God?! I know that You are sovereign and this has not caught You by surprise. But I also know that the king's heart is like channels of water in Your hand; You can turn it wherever You want, God. Help us!* With that, I silenced my cell phone, turned out the light, laid my head on the pillow, and drifted off with tears running down my cheeks and a sense of deep despair, not only for myself, my family, and my community, but for my country.

Lo and behold, the sun came up the next morning. Life goes on. But I sensed that with this new day, we had turned a new corner that would lead to suffering the likes of which I haven't seen in my lifetime. *Sigh.*

So what's changed for you? I heard from somewhere deep within my distraught heart. Before I got out of bed, the Lord had given me new perspective—life-altering perspective. "The only thing that has changed for you is that the fields just got a lot whiter!"

Behold, I say to you, lift up your eyes and look on the fields, that they are white for harvest. (John 4:35)

What a seemingly odd thing for Jesus to say to His disciples. Their travels had brought them to Jacob's well in Samaria, where Jesus had stopped to rest. While the disciples were off getting the evening meal, Jesus engaged in conversation with a Samaritan woman who had come to the well for water. Ultimately, He revealed to her that He is the long-awaited Messiah. She departed in haste, eager to tell the townspeople that the Promised One they had been waiting for had finally come (John 4:7–28).

As she returned to town with the exciting news, the disciples returned to the well with dinner. One can only imagine their facial expressions of shock and confusion. In first century Israel, it was taboo for a Jewish man to speak with a woman in public, much less a Samaritan woman whose people were deeply despised by the Jews, because they considered them half-breed pagans. Yet here is their Rabbi, Jesus, conversing with this off-limits female. Scandalous! And they don't even know the half of it, as she was also a woman of ill repute!

Though their faces must have reflected their dismay, not a word was said about the woman. Instead, they did what we all do in those uncomfortable situations—change the subject. "Rabbi, eat," they urged. The disciples' primary concern was their rumbling stomachs. Making it clear that this was not a time for eating and drinking and focusing on themselves, Jesus challenged His disciples to take their eyes off of their physical circumstances and see what He could see through a spiritual lens.

Jesus said to them, "My food is to do the will of Him who sent Me and to accomplish His work. Do you not say, 'There are yet four months, and then comes the harvest'? Behold, I say to you, lift up your eyes and look on the fields, that they are white for harvest." (John 4:34–35)

The natural harvest was still months off, so it is unlikely that Jesus was referring to the ripe-white crops in the field. Rather, it appears that He was drawing his disciples' attention to the white robes of townsmen making their way to the well. The people wanted to see for themselves if there was truth to the woman's report. Could this man—this Jewish Rabbi who dared to enter their marginalized community—be the Savior of the world?

The biblical text tells us that Jesus stayed in Samaria for two days, interacting with the people. John recorded that many more Samaritans believed because of the Messiah's teaching. "For we have heard for ourselves and know that this One is indeed the Savior of the world" (John 4:42). Jesus offered these marginalized people hope with the truth of the Gospel.

Political strife and chaos, Ebola, ISIS, lone-wolf terrorism, economic instability, racial tension, joblessness, homelessness, *hopelessness*. There is nothing I can do to change any of these modern-day circumstances. Except hopelessness. The only true and lasting solution for that is Jesus Christ, who is calling me and all of His followers to see this world—a world that seems to be spinning faster and faster out of control—as He sees it.

"The only thing that has changed for you is that the fields just got a lot whiter." That morning, as I awoke with an overwhelming sense of despair and fear for the future, God changed my perspective before my feet hit the cold floor. "Lift up your eyes, My daughter, and see what I see, more people ready and willing to turn to Me."

My job isn't to resolve all of the suffering that I see around me. My job is to give hurting people the hope of Jesus Christ. And that job gets bigger as the world spins further and further out of control with pain and suffering.

You and I may never be called to life-threatening service like caring for Ebola patients or serving refugees in Syria while ISIS continues its murderous rampage just a few miles away. But we are called to *life-giving* service in our families, neighborhoods, churches, communities, country, and world.

Behold, I say to you, lift up your eyes and look on the fields,
that they are white for harvest. (John 4:35)

If your gift is teaching, prepare to teach like you never have before. If your gift is giving, prepare to open your wallet like you never have before. If your gift is hospitality, prepare to open your doors like you never have before. Whatever your gifts, prepare to use them like you never have before. There is a time for weeping and a time for reaping. Now is the time for Christ-followers to look up, see the white fields of harvest, and reap!

Merciful God,
It is hard to see so much pain and suffering in the world.
I am so quick to say, "Lord, do something!"
when You already have done something.
By the blood of Your Son, You offer true, lasting hope
in seemingly hopeless situations.
And, by Your Spirit, You have empowered me
to tell people about You
and the hope that they, too, can have in You.
Father, give me the eyes to see opportunity
where most see fear and despair.
And give me the courage to act on that opportunity,
by sharing the Good News that You bring to all circumstances,
no matter how hopeless they seem.
In Christ's Name and for His glory and honor, I pray.
Amen.

CHAPTER 5

Basement Reflections on *Deception*

God and the Selfie Stick

The Legacy Lie

Blessed—The Hypocrisy of It

The Stinking Truth

God and the Selfie Stick

I've been told it's one of the greatest inventions in modern history: the selfie stick. One of *TIME* magazine's The 25 Best Inventions of 2014,[1] the selfie stick enables you to take your own picture from more than an arm's length away. The telescoping gadget has a handle on one end and a clamp on the other. Put your smartphone in the clamp, extend the stick to a desirable distance and angle, press a button, and *voilà*!

This global phenomenon has the French saying, *"Enough!"* The selfie stick, or "narcisstick" as some have labeled it, has been banned at the Palace of Versailles in Paris. Other attractions following suit include the National Gallery in London, the Colosseum in Rome, the Smithsonian in Washington, DC, and New York City's MoMA and the Met. Apparently people walking around with long poles, capturing themselves on camera while being oblivious to their surroundings, pose a bit of a hazard called selfie-inflicted injury. "The twirling around of hundreds of sticks can become unwittingly dangerous," said a spokesman for the Colosseum in Rome.[2]

Ya think? Unwittingly dangerous (and obnoxious I might add) in more ways than the obvious. I would argue that the "selfie" craze poses a *significant* threat to our spiritual lives. In a matter of seconds, we can snap a photo of ourselves and put it out on social media screaming, "Hey, look at me!" to the ends of the earth. And for some, one selfie isn't enough. There seems to be something seductively addictive about taking snapshot after snapshot of ourselves and posting them for the world to see.

Don't get me wrong. I love seeing photos of my friends in far off places enjoying wonderful adventures. But in this selfie-saturated world, where mankind will go to extreme lengths to capture our own images (including a Stretch Armstrong-like appendage[3] to photograph our best side), we have taken the idolatry that Paul wrote about in Romans to a whole new level.

> For although they knew God, they did not glorify him as God or give him thanks, but they became futile in their thoughts and their senseless hearts were darkened. Although they claimed to be wise, they became fools and exchanged the glory of the immortal God for an image resembling mortal human beings or birds or four-footed animals or reptiles. (Romans 1:21–23 NET)

Think about the Ten Commandments. What does God address first? Idolatry.

First Commandment: "You shall have no other gods before Me" (Exodus 20:3).

Second Commandment: "You shall not make for yourself an idol, or any likeness of what is in heaven above or on the earth beneath or in the water under the earth" (Exodus 20:4).

Why does idolatry top God's list? Because it impacts the very foundation of our worship. God knew the heart of man. And He knew man's desire to worship something that he could create and, therefore, control with his own hands. This is why *Yahweh* never revealed His own image to the Israelites in Exodus. He spoke to Moses from a burning bush. He traveled with His people in pillars of clouds and fire. When Moses boldly asked to see the His face, He covered Moses' eyes and let him see only His back passing by. And it was God's *Shekinah* glory that resided in the Holy of Holies. The Lord did not show His face because He knew that man would craft idols out of wood and stone in His likeness and worship them—man's creation—rather than the Creator.

It was not until God the Son wrapped himself in human flesh and humbly entered into our world that God the Father offered mankind an image of Himself. Jesus said,

> If you have known me, you will know my Father too. And from now on you do know him and have seen him. (John 14:7 NET)

And He is worthy of our worship ... because *He is God*!

By definition, an *idol* is something that is worshiped as a god or supreme being. In today's society, "self" is often held in higher esteem than the Savior. We have become our own "self-made" idols.

That might sound a bit harsh, but consider this: How many social media posts do we see about the Lord versus snapshots of ourselves on a daily basis? I don't want to throw cold water on social media's fun selfie fad (we saw enough of that with the ice bucket challenge). Go ahead and take a picture of yourself skydiving. What a great moment to capture and share! Buy that selfie stick so that you don't have to set up a camera and then run to join the family photo before the flash. It will make for a great Christmas card. But like anything else, moderation is key.

So how do you know when you've gone too far and this fun fad becomes dangerous idolatry of "self"? When your identity and security come from *your* selfie stick rather than *God's* selfie stick.

What is God's selfie stick, you ask? The stick on which His Son voluntarily died, paying the price for our sins so that we could have eternal life with Him. That, and that alone, is the selfie stick worth picking up moment by moment, day after day.

Creator God,
You created us in Your image.
We did not create You in our image.
And yet, it is our image that captures our attention.
We are deceived into thinking that if we draw
more attention to ourselves, we will be more special.
Yet, You tell us just how special we are in Your Word:
"When I consider Your heavens, the work of Your fingers,
The moon and the stars, which You have ordained;
What is man that You take thought of him,
And the son of man that You care for him?
Yet You have made him a little lower than God,
And You crown him with glory and majesty!" (Psalm 8:3–5).
Lord, it is my heart's desire to draw attention to You.
If every minute of a day were captured in photos,
I pray that in every snapshot, people would see You and not me.

You and You alone are worthy of our worship, my worship.
I love You, God.
In the Name of Your Son, Jesus Christ, my Savior.
Amen.

The Legacy Lie

During the summer of 2015, while I was recovering from pneumonia, I spent a lot of time on my patio enjoying the company of a regular visitor—a brave little doe that I affectionately call "Levi's Daughter" because of her strength and fearlessness. Who is Levi's daughter, you might ask? She is the birth mother of Moses. We read about her in the second chapter of Exodus.

Threatened by the ever-increasing Hebrew population, Pharaoh ordered that all baby boys be put to death. It was his sadistic way of trying to contain the development of the nation of Israel. But a young woman, identified only as "a daughter of Levi," kept her baby boy hidden for the first three months of his life. When he became too big to go unnoticed, she cleverly made him noticeable by placing him in a basket among the reeds of the Nile where Pharaoh's daughter bathed.

> And she saw the basket among the reeds and sent her maid, and she brought it to her. When she opened it, she saw the child, and behold, the boy was crying. And she had pity on him and said, "This is one of the Hebrews' children." (Exodus 2:5–6)

Imagine the courage it took this Hebrew mother to expose her infant son to a member of Pharaoh's family! There could be one of only two results—murder or mercy. As the true-life drama unfolded, Pharaoh's daughter mercifully took the child as her own, naming him Moses. This "Moses" would become the man God would choose to rescue His people from slavery in Egypt, a foreshadowing of the Savior to come who would deliver His people out of the bondage of sin. What a legacy we have received from Moses. His life foreshadowed the coming of Jesus Christ, which happened some twelve hundred years later.

But what about Moses' birth mother? Oh, my! If not for her bravery and trust in *Yahweh*, Moses would have perished with an entire generation of Hebrew boys. Her contribution to our spiritual heritage is an extraordinary legacy. And yet, *we have no record of her name.* It's not important to the story. It is her courage and faithfulness to *Yahweh* that is recorded in His Word.

Our culture often talks about legacy, how the world will remember certain folks. People at the pinnacle of politics, business, entertainment, and, yes, even the church are so hyper-focused on how they will be remembered that they forget why they have been given the privilege of leadership. They have been deceived into putting more thought and energy into making a name for themselves, rather than for the Lord.

A number of years ago, I was helping a parachurch organization with its communications strategy. It was my privilege to come alongside them in a new effort to advance their mission. I was particularly excited about a specific piece of the plan that would expand the ministry's message to audiences beyond their current reach. Having proven successful with other Kingdom-building efforts, this plan was enthusiastically received by the majority of the leadership team. But the head of the organization dug in his heels, vehemently opposing it.

"I don't want to put my legacy at risk," he declared. Nearing the end of his ministry career, he was consumed with how he would be remembered, and, therefore, he was risk averse. He had one primary objective: Preserve the integrity of his name.

I get it. No one wants to fall on their face when they're nearing the finish line. We all want to be "remembered well." And I admit, there is always risk in trying new things. But when our primary motivation is to build a name for ourselves, rather than the name of Christ, the glory of God is hijacked.

LORD, make me to know my end
And what is the extent of my days;
Let me know how transient I am.

Behold, You have made my days as handbreadths,
And my lifetime as nothing in Your sight;
Surely every man at his best is a mere breath.
Selah. (Psalm 39:4–5)

(Note that "Selah" is meant to cause us to pause and let what has been said sink in.)

"What is my legacy?" There is nothing wrong with the question. We all want to make a mark on this world and a name for ourselves. But if the desire for our own name to be known rises above the desire for His name to be known, it would be better if we weren't remembered at all. In his Letter to the Philippians, Paul wrote:

Instead of being motivated by selfish ambition or vanity, each of you should, in humility, be moved to treat one another as more important than yourself. Each of you should be concerned not only about your own interests, but about the interests of others as well. You should have the same attitude toward one another that Christ Jesus had, who though he existed in the form of God did not regard equality with God as something to be grasped, but emptied himself by taking on the form of a slave, by looking like other men, and by sharing in human nature. He humbled himself, by becoming obedient to the point of death—even death on a cross! As a result God highly exalted him and gave him the name that is above every name, so that at the name of Jesus every knee will bow—in heaven and on earth and under the earth—and every tongue confess that Jesus Christ is Lord to the glory of God the Father. (Philippians 2:3–11 NET)

Levi's daughter reminds us that some of the greatest legacies we have come from saints whose names we do not know. God used them mightily, and, down through the ages, generations have benefited from these anonymous lives well lived for the Lord.

So what will be your legacy? How do you hope future generations will remember you? By the glory you built for your name or for the name above all names? *Selah.*

Heavenly Father,
The Enemy has done a good job convincing us that
our lives matter only if we leave an admirable legacy,
a stamp on this world that has our name on it.
But Your Word tells us that it is only at the name of Jesus
that every knee will bow and every tongue confess
that He is Lord.
I bow right now before the name of Jesus
and acknowledge Him as my Savior.
It is by His Name that I want to be remembered.
Help me to live my life accordingly,
rejecting the lie that I have to do something great
to make a great name for myself and embracing the truth
that only One name ultimately matters—Jesus.
Let this be my legacy, that generations from now,
people will know Him because I lived in His Name.
Amen.

Blessed—The Hypocrisy of It

On a recent trip I lost one of my all-time favorite hats. It was a black, bedazzled ball cap embroidered with the claim "Blessed Beyond Measure." I loved it, not only because it turned a bad hair day into a cute hair day, but it told the world that I felt exceedingly blessed.

Liar.

I was studying the Gospel of Luke when I found myself lamenting the loss of my hat. By no coincidence, I was approaching the Beatitudes, which are a series of blessings taught by Jesus and recounted in the Gospel of Luke (Luke 6:20–26) and the Gospel of Matthew (Matthew 5:2–12). Coming to Luke 6:20, the word *blessed* jumped off the page.

> And turning His gaze toward His disciples, He began to say, "Blessed are you who are poor, for yours is the kingdom of God." (Luke 6:20)

Startled, I realized how quick I was to tell people I'm "blessed" when I hadn't really considered what that meant. The Greek word Luke uses for *blessed*, μακάριος (*makarios*), means "happy." (Note that this is a different word than the Greek word for *happiness* described in chapter 4.) The Hebrew equivalent, אַשְׁרֵי (*esher*), provides further dimension, implying bliss or satisfaction. As used by Jesus then, *blessed* means "to be blissfully happy, supremely content."

Does that describe me? On most days, no. I have had moments of happiness, even blissfulness from time to time. But do I exist in a constant state of supreme contentment? How I wish I could say yes.

Anyone who knows me well has heard me say, "I can't wait until I finally arrive at happy." I have long projected my happiness into the realm of "if." *If* I were more financially secure, then I would be content. *If* I had a husband to share my life, then I would be truly happy. *If* my ministry was bigger, or my waistline was smaller, then I would finally be satisfied.

But that's not what Jesus, the Creator of *happy*, is saying. His use of "blessed" in the Beatitudes refers to who (make that Whose) we are, not where we are in our achievement of personal goals.

The Greek noun for *poor* here, πτωχός (*ptóchos*), means "beggar." Certainly, the materially impoverished are in view here. Some of the happiest people I have ever known are Christ-followers in third world countries. With little more than nothing, they know that they are wholly and completely dependent on God for everything. And that translates into enviable bliss. But turn to the Gospel of Matthew and his account of the Beatitudes. Notice how Matthew adds further dimension to Jesus' statement.

> Blessed are the poor in spirit, for theirs is the kingdom of heaven. (Matthew 5:3)

The truly blessed people in this world are spiritual beggars, people who recognize they have nothing to offer God. In turn, they seek Him with humility and satisfaction, knowing He will supply their every need.

And pause for a minute to really give this some thought: In the majority of the Beatitudes, Christ sets our expectations in the future tense. "They shall be comforted." "They shall inherit the earth." "They shall be satisfied." And so on.

But He uses the present tense in the first Beatitude. "For theirs is the kingdom of heaven." Complete dependence on Him in the here and now translates into present-day happy! We all expect to be deliriously happy when we get to Heaven. But Jesus is saying that we don't have to wait. Eternally-existent, supreme contentment is available now, if we will just trust that He knows our needs better than we do and that He will meet those needs in ways we cannot.

My favorite place on the planet is the wilderness of Israel. Stark and desolate, nothing can grow on its own in the vast desert expanse south of Jerusalem. Survival in the wilderness requires complete dependence on God. And I have never known a place where I feel more alive. I can certainly see myself wearing my "Blessed Beyond Measure" hat there (if anyone finds it).

In the meantime, I have a second "Blessed" hat, one with more subtlety and no bling. I have wondered if I should hang it up until I can wear it with authenticity. Admittedly, I am not yet supremely content with the life God has given to me. But I have decided to don the ball cap anyway—not to tell people I have a great life, but to remind myself that I have a great God, and, without Him, I have and am nothing.

O taste and see that the LORD is good;
How blessed is the man who takes refuge in Him! (Psalm 34:8)

My God,
Giver of every good thing,
You have blessed me beyond measure.
That is truth!
You have given me life, and life eternal,
through Your Son, Jesus Christ.
And, oh, how often I take that for granted, Lord.
Forgive me.
By Your Spirit, help me to be a spiritual beggar,
recognizing that I have nothing to offer You,
the Creator of the Universe.
But You have so much to offer me, like peace and joy,
if I would humbly seek my satisfaction in You and not the world.
Lord, You promise that You will provide for my every need.
And You have assured me
that You will never leave or forsake me.
How could I possibly ask for anything more?
Father, I am truly Blessed Beyond Measure.
I love You and give thanks to You,
my Creator, my Provider, my Savior.
In Jesus' Name and for His glory and honor.
Amen.

The Stinking Truth

One day as I was vacuuming my bedroom, I stumbled over the cord and flew headlong into the wall, landing in a crumpled, unconscious mess on the floor. I don't know how long I was out (probably just a few seconds), but when I came to, I discovered that an ugly, black-and-blue knot had risen on my forehead. Worse, ugly thoughts and emotions had started to rise up in my heart and mind.

No one even knows I'm here! I suddenly realized. I had lived alone as a single woman for years. But somehow, it never occurred to me how "alone" I was until I lay sprawled out on the floor in pain. *If I died, no one would know it until I started to stink!* I whined. As the panic and fear rose in my heart, I threw a full-on, adult-sized tantrum aimed directly at God.

"If You had given me a husband, I wouldn't be in a situation like this!" I shouted loud enough to reach the heavens. It wasn't that I needed a spouse to do the vacuuming. My ridiculous reasoning was that if I had a husband when I died, at least he would find my corpse before I started to stink. Apparently, someone above heard me, because what came next sounded like roars of laughter. It was as if the heavens opened up and out of them bellowed, "Bahahahaha!"

I can envision the apostle Paul in stitches, doubled over in amusement. In his Letter to the Philippians, Paul warned of the threat of false teaching in the church. Lies about life in the Lord had started to seep into Paul's favorite congregation. "Evil workers," as he called them, were corrupting the Gospel with the idea that true happiness was rooted in the world and man's selfish, "fleshly" desires. Paul countered, encouraging the Philippians to find their joy *in the Lord* and not the world.

> Rejoice in the Lord always; again I will say, rejoice! Let your gentle spirit be known to all men. The Lord is near. Be anxious for nothing, but in everything by prayer and supplication with thanksgiving let your requests be made known to God. And the peace of God, which surpasses all comprehension, will guard your hearts and your minds in Christ Jesus. (Philippians 4:4–7)

If anyone would know about worldly satisfaction, it would be Paul. Before his conversion, Paul was among Israel's elite—well-educated, wealthy, influential, rapidly climbing the ladder of success. This was a guy who had it all and was gaining hero status among the Jews for his persecution of Christ-followers. Then Christ got ahold of him on the road to Damascus, and the apostle's life was never the same.

Submitting to Christ, Paul gave up *everything* he had previously valued— fame, fortune, success. But he gained the transformative understanding of true *joy*. It's not found in things of this world. True joy is found in the Lord. And Christ-followers need to hold on to that truth with everything that they have, lest they trip over the lies of the Enemy who seeks to convince us that God is not enough. When we buy into the lie that God is cruelly withholding the thing that would give us true joy, we are at risk of flying headlong into spiritual disobedience.

I think it's pretty obvious what was going on in my heart that day when I stumbled over the vacuum cord. I had bought into the lie that true joy is found in earthly desires (like marriage), and I took a spiritual tumble that I never want to repeat. If I had sought joy in the Lord, I would have responded with something like, *Wow, this really hurts. But thank You, Lord, for protecting me from worse injury. And thank You for being here with me, even though I feel so alone."*

Instead, while I was still unconscious (maybe even while I was flying through the air), the Enemy was whispering in my ear: "Poor, pitiful you. God didn't give you a husband, and now you are going to die alone and stink!" You know what really stinks? That I believed him!

I wish I had remembered another woman who found herself in a precarious situation without a husband—Mary. When God told her that she was about to become a young, unwed, pregnant teen in a culture where that could get you stoned to death, she responded with joy.

> And Mary said:
> "My soul exalts the Lord,
> And my spirit has rejoiced in God my Savior.
> "For He has had regard for the humble state of His bondslave;
> For behold, from this time on all generations will count me
> blessed." (Luke 1:46–48)

Mary trusted in the Lord's plan and provision for her life, and that gave her great joy.

Fortunately, as I lay there on the floor, looking up and seeing nothing but pity, it didn't take me long to come to my spiritual senses and see the absurdity in my tantrum. I rejoiced in the Lord with a good belly laugh of my own. God is faithful and ever-present. Trusting Him will always lead to peace of mind and heart, and sometimes a good laugh.

"Rejoice in the Lord always; again I will say, rejoice!"

Lord God,
When I throw tantrums over my life circumstances,
I deserve nothing but Your contempt.
In my heart, I have bought the lie
that things would be a lot better
if You would just give me what I want.
Thank You, Lord, for being a good and loving Father
who knows what I need and withholds no good thing from me.
I am certain that Satan will continue to try
to convince me that life could be better
if You, Lord, would just submit to my plan.
Father, I submit myself to Your plan for my life
and I pray that, as the Enemy is whispering
lies in my ear, the Spirit will shout in my heart,
"God is good! Rejoice in the Lord!"
You, and You alone, are worthy of my praise, worship, and trust.
In the Name of Jesus Christ, for His glory and honor, I pray.
Amen.

CHAPTER 6

Basement Reflections
on
the Holy-days

Caught in the New Year's Gap

As the calendar turns the page at year's end, we traditionally look back on the past twelve months, counting our blessings, lamenting our blunders, and moving forward into the New Year with fresh hope and anticipation. But I sometimes find myself caught in what I call the New Year's Gap—too weary to look back on what was a difficult and painful year and too afraid to look ahead, dreading what the New Year might or might not bring.

It's a familiar place—this New Year's Gap. On January 1, 2013, I wrote the following in my journal: "It hurts too much to look back. And I'm too afraid to look ahead into the unknown. I am … stuck."

Similar sentiments of being "stuck" met me at the starting line of recent years as well. One could argue that if I had enough faith, I would charge into the New Year with bold anticipation. In years past I have been able to do that, and hopefully, I will do so again. But for now, I have come to appreciate the New Year's Gap as a place where I meet the Lord with raw, gut-level honesty and He responds with truth that sets a spiritual course for the coming months.

One year, the Lord met me in the New Year's Gap with Psalm 78, a record of Israel's wilderness wanderings. In hindsight, the Lord was preparing me for my own wilderness wanderings and reminding me that He will never leave or forsake me.

As I entered another New Year, the Lord took more of a "tough love" approach with me on New Year's Day, leading me to Peter's denial (John 18:17–18) and the question: Would I embrace or deny Him in the face of fear? In hindsight, the Lord wasn't breaking me down but building me up for a year of faith-rocking experiences.

And then there was the year when I prayed, "Lord, all I want is a year of peace, joy, and restoration."

God's response: The soldier, the athlete, and the farmer.

So you, my child, be strong in the grace that is in Christ Jesus. ...
Take your share of suffering as a good soldier of Christ Jesus.
No one in military service gets entangled in matters of everyday
life; otherwise he will not please the one who recruited him.
Also, if anyone competes as an athlete, he will not be crowned
as the winner unless he competes according to the rules. The
farmer who works hard ought to have the first share of the crops.
(2 Timothy 2:1, 3–6 NET)

In his Second Letter to Timothy, Paul encourages his young mentee to press on. The apostle imparts wisdom that is specifically related to vocational ministry. However, the deep truth in Paul's counsel is valuable to Christ-followers in all walks of life.

Paul says, "Be strong in the grace that is in Christ Jesus." In other words, don't rely on your own strength. As Christ-followers, we are equipped with the power of divine grace. Paul tells Timothy to leverage that power and allow it to provide the motivation and strength needed to serve the Lord, even in tough times. As one who has long relied on (and even taken pride in) my own power, this concept of strength in the Lord does not come easy. What, exactly, does strength in the Lord look like?

First, Paul says it looks like an active duty *soldier*. "Take your share of suffering as a good soldier of Christ Jesus. No one in military service gets entangled in matters of everyday life; otherwise he will not please the one who recruited him" (verses 3–4).

I can't help but think of US Navy SEAL Chris Kyle, whose heroism is recounted in the book and movie *American Sniper*. Over his four tours of duty in Iraq, Kyle became the most lethal sniper in US military history. *Focused. Undistracted. Single-minded. Obedient.* These are the characteristics that made Chris Kyle a fierce warrior and empowered him to do his job so well. Paul points to these attributes when he says that operating in the strength of the Lord looks like a soldier equipped for battle.

Next, Paul points to an *athlete*. "If anyone competes as an athlete, he will not be crowned as the winner unless he competes according to the rules" (verse 5).

Paul has the Roman games (ancient, Olympic-style competition) in view. To win the victor's crown, an athlete would have had to appropriately prepare for competition and do nothing to disqualify himself (i.e. cheating). *Disciplined. Self-Controlled. Principled.* These are the characteristics Paul points to when he tells Timothy that operating in the strength of the Lord looks like an athlete preparing for victory.

Finally, Paul points to a *farmer.* "The farmer who works hard ought to have the first share of the crops" (verse 6).

If you have spent any time on a farm or ranch, you know the kind of exhausting, backbreaking effort that is required. A crop ripens out of hard work, not laziness. The farmer's reward? The harvest, when he is first in line to collect his fair share. *Diligent. Hardworking. Committed.* These are the characteristics Paul points to when he tells Timothy that operating in the strength of the Lord looks like a farmer.

The soldier. The athlete. The farmer. Nothing about these figures implies ease or comfort. The apostle's point: Serving the Lord is not for the faint of heart. But there's more if we dive deeper into the text.

Think about what I am saying and the Lord will give you understanding of all this. (2 Timothy 2:7 NET)

Notice what goes unsaid in this verse but speaks volumes into our walk with Christ. A soldier serves his commander. An athlete trusts his trainer. And a successful farmer relies on rain for the harvest. It is the power of another that equips and motivates us.

So if you find yourself in the New Year's Gap, be strong in the Lord— serving, trusting, and relying on Him. He is the only One who can look down the road and see what is coming your way. Hardship or happiness, tragedy or triumph, despair or delight. He is fully aware of your needs and will equip and empower you for whatever lies ahead.

Lord,
You are not a God who stands back
and watches His children squirm.

You are a faithful and loving Father who refines us in the fire.
I pray that the months to come
will bring reprieve from my struggles.
And, oh Lord, how I would love fun, new adventures.
But even if things get worse before they get better,
I know that You will equip me to endure the struggle
and empower me to honor and glorify You
in the midst of the struggle.
You are my strength and my shield.
My heart trusts in You, and I am helped.
Thank You for loving me like You do.
In the Name of Your Son, my Savior Jesus Christ.
Amen.

What's That He Said?

He is RISEN! Hallelujah! Now what?

On Tuesday, two days after Resurrection Sunday, Easter is behind us for another year. Aside from a few Easter remnants—leftover ham, half-eaten chocolate bunnies, and a laundry basket filled with pastel party clothes—it's just Tuesday. Time to get back to business. Right?

But wait ... shouldn't our lives look a little different (maybe even *profoundly* different) on the Tuesday after Easter? After we have boldly claimed and proclaimed the astonishing, stupefying, mind-blowing truth that Jesus Christ, Son of God, God Himself died for us and then rose from the dead! But that was two days ago. Time to get back to business as usual.

I don't know about you, but I sure could use some inspiration about now, maybe even more so *after* Easter when, in the shadow of the Cross, the world around us returns to "normal."

"ELI, ELI, LEMA SABACHTHANI?" that is, "MY GOD, MY GOD, WHY HAVE YOU FORSAKEN ME?" (Matthew 27:46)

Yes! That's exactly what I needed to hear! The words of Jesus right before His death.

I know, an odd choice for a spiritual boost. But if you were a Jew at the foot of the Cross in that dark, dark hour, you would not have heard a desperate cry to a callous God. You would have heard a reminder that *Yahweh* is sovereign and holy, that He is faithful to His people, that He is the Creator God who purposefully brings His children into the world. You would have been assured that despite the way things appear, the Lord is near and will deliver His people. And you would have heard that Jesus is the Messiah who was prophesied in the Hebrew Scriptures.

You see, when Jesus uttered, "My God, my God, why have You forsaken Me," He was quoting Psalm 22:1. And He wasn't proof-texting (using that verse out of context) to describe His personal feelings of abandonment. He was invoking the whole of Psalm 22 to testify to God's faithfulness.

If I say to you, "The Lord is my shepherd, I shall not want," what is your next thought? Most likely, "He makes me lie down in green pastures; He leads me beside quiet waters." Right? We recognize Psalm 23 in the first verse, which triggers a recall of the whole psalm.

In the first century, the Psalter (The Book of Psalms) served as a worship hymnal for the Nation of Israel. Jews were intimately familiar with *all* of the psalms and could recall any psalm with just a few words. So, when Jesus quoted Psalm 22:1 from the Cross, the entirety of Psalm 22—all thirty-one verses—would have come to mind for those watching Him die, friends *and foes*. And they would have recalled a song of confidence and hope in the Lord, as Psalm 22 volleys human despair back and forth with divine truth.

My God, my God, why have You forsaken me?
Far from my deliverance are the words of my groaning.
O my God, I cry by day, but You do not answer;
And by night, but I have no rest.
Yet You are holy,
O You who are enthroned upon the praises of Israel. (verses 1–3)

But I am a worm and not a man,
A reproach of men and despised by the people.
All who see me sneer at me;
They separate with the lip, they wag the head, saying,
"Commit yourself to the LORD; let Him deliver him;
Let Him rescue him, because He delights in him." (verse 6–8)

Yet You are He who brought me forth from the womb;
You made me trust when upon my mother's breasts. (verse 9)

Additionally, this exquisite Psalm of David is a messianic psalm, prophesying the very scene of the crucifixion a thousand years prior to Christ's death.

> I am poured out like water,
> And all my bones are out of joint;
> My heart is like wax;
> It is melted within me.
> My strength is dried up like a potsherd,
> And my tongue cleaves to my jaws;
> And You lay me in the dust of death.
> For dogs have surrounded me;
> A band of evildoers has encompassed me;
> They pierced my hands and my feet.
> I can count all my bones.
> They look, they stare at me;
> They divide my garments among them,
> And for my clothing they cast lots. (verses 14–18)

So when He uses His last gulps of breath to quote from Psalm 22, Jesus is telling us that *Yahweh* is a Promise Keeper, and the promise of a Savior is fulfilled in *Him*!

Read Psalm 22, all of it. See the messianic promise fulfilled in Christ. Recognize that Jesus' final words were about hope, not despair and abandonment (despite the appearance of such). Embrace the promise of a coming kingdom that will overcome *all* suffering and unrighteousness. Jesus' words, "My God, My God, why have You forsaken Me?" were intended to encourage believers who were watching their Lord die, and to terrify persecutors who would see an empty tomb. Today, they inspire us to not only rejoice in His resurrection, but to live victoriously through His Word in the day to day.

Now that's a message that will preach on Tuesday.

Lord,
Your Word delights my heart and stirs my soul.
It is better to me than thousands of gold and silver pieces.

Thank You that when we dive deep below the surface of Scripture,
we discover limitless caches of Your Character and Truth.
And thank You, Lord, that Your Word
became flesh and dwelt among us.
From the Cross, a weapon created
to terrify and discourage Your people,
we hear His cries of victory, not defeat.
He affirms who You are, a sovereign and holy God
who is faithful to His people and keeps His promises.
You have promised eternal life.
And I can look forward to the day when I enter into Your presence.
You have promised that Christ will come again.
And we can have confidence that, one day, that too will happen.
You are good and trustworthy and faithful to Your Word.
Hallelujah!
Amen.

Ta-Da!

It was a Saturday afternoon and I had settled into my comfy chair by the window, enjoying the changing colors of autumn and the occasional deer or rabbit passing by. The perfect opportunity to catch up on some reading and spend some time with the Lord.

Squeals and giggles from down the hall broke the silence every now and then, causing a smile to break across my face. The sounds of little girls playing "dress up" are music to a loving aunt's ears.

At some point while I was deep in thought, I unwittingly became the "audience" rather than an eavesdropper. "Ta-da!" my nieces shouted as they struck a pose in front of me. Wrapped in sequins and feathers, gowns and gloves, colorful bracelets and strings of pearls, and, of course, sparkly tiaras, my precious kiddos had delighted themselves by diving into the "dress up" chest that their nana and I put together for them not long before. Proud as peacocks (and looking a bit like our feathered friends as well), these precious little girls practically glowed with the joy of transformation and the grand appearance they had just made before me.

"Ta-da!" It's an expression that seems to explode with surprise and joy as it pulls the curtain back and something remarkable appears. *Ta-da* is truly one of my favorite expressions, and I have often used it over the years to announce accomplishment or transformation in my life. I love it! I think that may have something to do with my love for תּוֹדָה (*todah*), the Hebrew word for "thanksgiving."

I will sing praises to God's name!
I will magnify him as I give him thanks [*todah*]!
(Psalm 69:30 NET)

In Ancient Israel a *todah* was an offering of thanksgiving to God for an answer to prayer or deliverance from dire circumstances. It's a bit like the Thanksgiving we celebrate in America. A feast honoring the Lord is prepared, and the host invites friends and family to join them in giving thanks for God's abundant blessings. But in Ancient Israel the *todah* was not limited to once a year. It took place any time someone wanted to publicly proclaim their gratitude to the Lord for His blessings. Unique in that it is the only sacrificial offering that was allowed to be consumed by the offerer and his friends and family, the *todah* was quite a party!

Let's enter his presence with thanksgiving [*todah*]!
Let's shout out to him in celebration! (Psalm 95:2 NET)

What I love most about the *todah* is that the one who is giving thanks to the Lord makes a big, public deal of it, recounting the circumstances from which he was delivered and the way in which God rescued him.

In America we tend to shy away from public spectacles that shine a big light on our troubles and struggles. People might find out that we're vulnerable and imperfect (as if that's some sort of a secret). So we quietly rejoice in our triumphs, so as not to draw attention to our tribulation. I think we can learn a thing or two from the Israelites who shined light on their problems so they could shine a bigger light on their God who resolved their problems.

So here's what I propose: Let's not limit ourselves to Thanksgiving this year. Let's host *todah* (or "giving thanks") celebrations year-round. Whenever the Lord rescues us from peril or struggle, or when He answers a prayer with His exceeding abundance (i.e. a new job, the sale of a home, the restoration of a marriage, sobriety), let's be bold and tell people just how remarkable He is. That may require some transparency and vulnerability, because people need to know the bad in order to truly appreciate the good. But just think how exciting it will be to draw the curtains back on our messy lives and shout "ta-da" (or *todah*), revealing the glory of our truly remarkable and faithful God.

Merciful God,
Giver of all good things,
You are worthy of a todah every day of my life,
as I am blessed to live out my days
with the hope that conquers all despair.
Forgive me when I have allowed the todah moments
to pass by because I am too ashamed, too prideful,
or too busy to acknowledge Your daily deliverance.
Lord, I want to live out this life You have given me
with the joy and enthusiasm of a little girl playing dress-up
who is excited to show off her transformation.
Every day, You dress me in Your Son's robes of righteousness,
and the transformation is nothing short of a miracle.
Help me show that to the world, not for my glory but for Yours.
In the Name of the One who will show the world
the ta-da of all ta-das when He returns
and puts His feet on the Mount of Olives.
Amen.

Night-LIGHT

The longest night of the year, otherwise known as the winter solstice. It is an astronomical phenomenon. But I marvel at the miracle it points to each and every year. Just as darkness gets its tightest grip on the world, the Light of the world bursts through!

> Then Jesus again spoke to them, saying, "I am the Light of the world; he who follows Me will not walk in the darkness, but will have the Light of life." (John 8:12)

I don't think it's any coincidence that we observe Christmas within days of marking the longest night of the year. We don't have biblical record of the exact date of Jesus' birth. But it appears to have first been celebrated on December 25 in the fourth century. The December 25 date may have been strategically chosen for its proximity to the winter solstice, an event that gave cause for great festivals among ancient pagans who worshiped the sun for overcoming the darkness. How appropriate that Christ-followers would employ this same time to celebrate the Truth that, indeed, the *Son* did conquer darkness!

> In him was life, and the life was the light of mankind. And the light shines on in the darkness, but the darkness has not mastered it. (John 1:4–5 NET)

It's an extraordinary image, isn't it? Our Savior—the Light that could not be dimmed by darkness! I challenge any Christ-follower to ponder the metaphor and not see Christ and Christmas in a new way.

Light—what is it? To a child who is afraid of the dark, it is comfort. To a night-traveler, it illumines the path home. On a cold day it provides warmth for a weary soul, and it awakens the senses. A bright light exposes danger and wickedness. A flashing light cautions us to move carefully. Light is a catalyst, kick-starting photosynthesis, which ultimately produces food for creation. And light is an energy source, powering modern-day technology. Though we rarely stop to recognize it, light is critical to our everyday lives. We would not survive without it, without Him. No wonder when God spoke Creation into existence, He did so first with *light.*

> In the beginning God created the heavens and the earth. The earth was formless and void, and darkness was over the surface of the deep, and the Spirit of God was moving over the surface of the waters. Then God said, "Let there be light"; and there was light. God saw that the light was good; and God separated the light from the darkness. (Genesis 1:1–4)

Sadly the Bible tells us that it wasn't long before spiritual darkness overcame the world. Despite his God-given ingenuity, man could not create a light strong enough to penetrate the inky black of his disobedient heart. He could not illuminate his own way back to God. He was lost …

Until the Lord Himself, in all of His mercy and glory, pierced through the darkness of the longest night.

> Magi from the east arrived in Jerusalem, saying, "Where is He who has been born King of the Jews? For we saw His star in the east and have come to worship Him." … And the star, which they had seen in the east, went on before them until it came and stood over the place where the Child was. When they saw the star, they rejoiced exceedingly with great joy. (Matthew 2:1–2, 9–10)

Light overcame their darkness! Light conquers our longest night! As the Lord illumines your path to the manger this Christmas, you may be distracted by the shadows of the world: depression, illness, financial distress, family dysfunction, senseless violence, political confusion, global chaos. But on the longest night, look up. See the stars and know that God is here.

"THE PEOPLE WHO WERE SITTING IN DARKNESS SAW A GREAT LIGHT, AND THOSE WHO WERE SITTING IN THE LAND AND SHADOW OF DEATH, UPON THEM A LIGHT DAWNED." From that time, Jesus began to preach and say, "Repent, for the kingdom of heaven is at hand." (Matthew 4:16–17)

The Light of the world has come and promises to come again. Let us rejoice!

Arise, shine; for your light has come,
And the glory of the LORD has risen upon you.
For behold, darkness will cover the earth
And deep darkness the peoples;
But the LORD will rise upon you
And His glory will appear on you. (Isaiah 60:1–2)

Merry Christmas to all, and to all a bright night!

Heavenly Father,
It truly blows my mind that You spoke light
into existence, and that light was Your first step
in bringing peace to a dark and chaotic cosmos.
And again, You sent Your Son, the Light of the World,
to rescue us from our chaos and darkness.
Forgive me for allowing the darkness to
strike terror in my heart and bring gloom to my days.
By Your Spirit,
strengthen me to boldly persevere through the darkness of life,
confident in the knowledge that it cannot overcome the Light.
The Lord is my light and my salvation; whom shall I fear?

You are my Light, my Hope, my Truth, my Peace, my Love—
my Christmas.
In the Name of Your Son, Jesus Christ,
who humbled Himself to birth in a stable
and death on the Cross for me.
Amen.

A Red Poppy New Year

The calendar says it's time for a fresh beginning. But two weeks into the New Year, I'm still trying to get off the starting block. Sound familiar? My problem is that I'm still exhausted from the holidays. In part because I spent more energy faking "merry" than making "merry" through the Christmas season. Truth be told, most days in December I just wanted to cry—a lot.

Experts say the holidays magnify grief. I can affirm that. Maybe you can too. More than any other time of the year, we miss those we have lost to death. But worse, I think, may be what we have lost to life: relationships, dreams, jobs, homes, promises.

If you are burdened with that kind of loss—the loss you cannot bury—I hope my vision for this New Year is an encouragement to you.

In your mind's eye imagine a field of poppy flowers. Big, bright red poppies as far as the eye can see! That's what a Canadian military doctor was looking at when he crafted one of the greatest wartime poems ever written.[1]

> *In Flanders fields the poppies blow*
> *Between the crosses, row on row,*
> *That mark our place; and in the sky*
> *The larks, still bravely singing, fly*
> *Scarce heard amid the guns below.*
> —*John McCrae, 1915*[2]

In the spring of 1915, during World War I, Lieutenant-Colonel John McCrae wrote "In Flanders Fields" as he gazed out over the Belgian landscape littered with the casualties of war. Amid the graves of his fallen comrades, Lieutenant-Colonel McCrae noticed blooms of poppies. Delicate flowers sprouting up in bright red abundance! It was an astonishing sight, because months earlier, during the bleakness of winter, the only red that covered the European countryside was the crimson blood of the wounded and dead. But in this new season, vibrant red sprang up with joy and hope, not grief.

The poppies didn't replace death. Soldiers still lay in their graves while friends and loved ones, including Lieutenant-Colonel McCrae, grieved their losses. But death was no longer all that could be seen. Life, in all of its magnificent glory, flourished between the graves.

The thief comes only to steal and kill and destroy; I came that they may have life, and have it abundantly. (John 10:10)

Just before Christmas, I was deeply grieving the loss of a family relationship. After years of trying to restore it, I had come to accept the truth that it was gone. All that was left of this once beloved bond was a deep hole in my heart, a wound swollen with anger, sorrow, and bitterness. As "the most wonderful time of the year" approached, the overwhelming sadness seemed more than I could bear. Dropping to my knees, I asked the Lord to fill the void with something that didn't hurt so much. *Lord, fill this hole with You,* I begged. *I don't know what that looks like. But I know I don't want resentment and sorrow to emanate from my heart this Christmas. I want You.* And instantly, behind the flood of tears, I envisioned bright red poppies bursting forth. The grave of that dead relationship was still there in my heart. And I could still feel the ache of the loss. But alongside it bloomed God's glory!

Did you know that the seeds of field poppies can lie dormant underground for years? It is only when the earth above them is tilled that they germinate and grow into flowers. During that horrendous winter of 1914–1915, trench warfare brutalized the ground of Flanders fields. On the surface all that Lieutenant-Colonel McCrae could see was death. But deep underground, as the soil was plowed by fierce combat, poppies were taking root. And in their time, God's time, they burst forth in praise of their Creator.

Life with Christ follows the same cycle. It can be a battle with severe casualties. But when we are honest about our pain and willing to *cede* the battlegrounds of our hearts to Him, He promises to *seed* our lives with abundant joy.

Those who sow in tears shall reap with joyful shouting.
He who goes to and fro weeping, carrying his bag of seed,
Shall indeed come again with a shout of joy,
bringing his sheaves with him. (Psalm 126:5–6)

Friends, God is seeding our lives for His glory. There are seasons when the battlefields of our hearts are littered with grief and loss. But we can be confident that the Lord is working underneath all that pain, preparing our hearts for praise. Like me, you may be in a brutal season of lament now. But be of good courage, the poppies are coming!

Wishing you a Red Poppy New Year!

My Good and Loving God,
Only in Your economy can the ravages of war seed life.
Lord, my heart aches with loss and grief.
But by the blood of Your Son, You bring life from death.
And I am crying out to You now
to turn the battleground of my heart
into a spectacular garden of hopeful blooms.
For Your glory and honor.
Amen.

CHAPTER 7

Basement
Reflections
on
*Peace with
the Lord*

Peace Be With You

God's Restraining Order

If He Came to Bring Peace, Why the Sword?

R.I.P.

Peace Be With You

What were the first words the Risen Christ spoke to His disciples? "Peace be with you." Most of us fly by that so quickly, with barely a passing glance. Maybe because it comes after the exhausting roller coaster ride of Easter when our emotions sink into a dark grave of grief and then rise to the jubilant heights of Heaven. I don't know about you, but when I come to the passage *after* the empty tomb, I seem to drift into a spiritual coma.

Wake up!

Christ's story doesn't end at the empty tomb. It's just beginning, and you don't want to miss it.

> So when it was evening on that day, the first day of the week, and when the doors were shut where the disciples were, for fear of the Jews, Jesus came and stood in their midst and said to them, "Peace be with you." And when He had said this, He showed them both His hands and His side. The disciples then rejoiced when they saw the Lord. So Jesus said to them again, "Peace be with you; as the Father has sent Me, I also send you." And when He had said this, He breathed on them and said to them, "Receive the Holy Spirit." (John 20:19–22)

Try to put yourself into that scene, maybe as a fly on the wall. The disciples are fearfully huddled together behind locked doors. They know that the bloodthirsty Jews who persecuted their Rabbi are now looking for them. Every creak in the house makes them jump. Anything that might sound like footsteps approaching the door sends shivers up their spines. And suddenly Jesus appears on the scene. "Peace be with you," He says, not once but twice.

When I recently took the time to put myself in that terror-filled room, I was astonished at Jesus' first words. Of all the statements He could have made, why "Peace be with you"? This greeting was a fairly common, informal salutation of the time that casually expressed a wish for well-being. But was this a casual meeting between Christ and His followers? Hardly! It is one of Christ's first appearances after His resurrection. The Lord is suddenly standing in bodily form, on the inside of locked doors, addressing a group of folks who are scared out of their gourds, wondering if they will meet the same fate as their leader.

If Hollywood were writing the script, Jesus would have said something like, "I'm back!" as He swooped in to save the day and rescue His disciples from the wicked men who were hunting them. But Hollywood isn't the owner of this story (thankfully), and Jesus does not rescue them from their tribulation. He does something even more astounding. He enters into it and offers His scarred hands to help them through it.

True peace isn't found in the *absence* of trouble. It is found in the *presence* of the Lord. And as we learn in the passage above, peace is connected to two very specific things: the wounds Christ bears and the breath of life He breathes.

Peace in the wounds. The first time Jesus says "Peace be with you" to His disciples, He shows them His crucifixion wounds. Why? What is the relationship between trauma caused by the most violent death in human history and "peace"? The wounds show that Christ is real! He was crucified. He died. And He rose from the dead. These horrific scars testify to the exquisitely beautiful Truth that He is who He says He is. The Savior of the world died and rose again. It's true! Oh the peace that comes from knowing He is trustworthy.

Peace in the breath. The second time Jesus says "Peace be with you" to His disciples, He breathes on them. Why? What is the association between "peace" and breath? Just as God breathed life into the nostrils of the first man (Genesis 2:7), enabling man to fellowship with Him, Christ breathes new life into His followers, enabling them (sinners) to have restored fellowship with God. Oh the peace that comes from knowing He enables us to live faithfully in this world and to live eternally with God!

With His wounded hands and His life-giving breath, Jesus demonstrates beyond a shadow of a doubt that He is King over death and life. And when those of us who have placed our faith in Him get that, when that Truth sinks into the marrow of our bones and the strands of our DNA, the result is peace. True peace.

Over the past several years, I have not lived in peace. I have lived in fear for months on end, sheer terror at times. But not too long ago, I heard that still, small voice in my heart say, "It's over. This season of fear is done." My heart swelled with excitement! I was certain that the Lord was finally going to free me from the circumstances that had terrorized me for so long!

But as it turns out, the Lord didn't rescue me out of my situation. He entered into it and did something even greater. He enabled me to see His wounds of death and fill my lungs with His breath of life. "Peace be with you," I hear Him saying to my broken heart. That's not a casual greeting. That's an eternal promise. Finally I am ready to receive it. Are you?

Oh Lord,
How is peace possible in the midst of fear and despair?
How do I move confidently and calmly
through my life when I am terrified of who
or what might be just around the corner?
By placing my hands in the scarred hands of Jesus,
that's how.
Submitting my fear and anxiety to the One
who died and rose from the grave,
the One who claimed victory over wickedness and death,
the One who now holds out
His wounded, faithful hands to me.
What an extraordinary "aha" moment when I heard
for the first time what Jesus really said.
"Peace be with you." You are peace!
And You are with me, forever. Wow.
Lord, I know myself well enough to know that
I will allow fear and anxiety to drain the peace
from my life again, and again, and again.
Please forgive me.

When that happens, mercifully whisper into my heart
those four life-changing words:
Peace be with you.
In the Name of Your Son, Jesus Christ,
my Savior and my Prince of Peace.
Amen.

God's Restraining Order

Just when you think the world has gone mad, you find out the world has gone well past mad to stark raving lunacy!

Man seeks restraining order against God
Haifa resident asks court to keep the Almighty away,
claiming He is being mean to him.
The Times of Israel, May 4, 2016[1]

I kid you not; this is a *real* story. Some guy actually petitioned a court to issue a restraining order against God! What do you do with that? I mean, writing on this craziness could go in so many directions. Oh, the possibilities!

But I want to focus on the topic of restraining orders. It just so happens that God has been teaching me a lot on the subject. Someone I love has recently had to petition a court for an order of protection. It is a terrifying process. In this particular state, you first have to stand before a judge and recount the trauma that prompted your petition. Next, you have to come face to face with the person who filled your life with terror. And then, if (and that's a big "if") a judge grants your request, you are handed a piece of paper stating that the person in question—the one who has rocked your world with fear—has to stay 100 feet away from you. That's it. No bodyguard. No round-the-clock surveillance. No assurance that this person will never hurt you again. Just a piece of paper that you are supposed to hand to the police if the most wicked person you know comes near. Not exactly comforting is it? And yet, it's all we have to give us peace.

Or is it?

Come to find out, God issues restraining orders as well. But the Lord's orders of protection aren't written on paper, and they don't come from the hand of a human judge. They are written in the Book of Life. They are offered by the pierced and bloodied hands of the One who has claimed victory over death. And they extend well beyond 100 feet, into eternity.

> And when you heard the word of truth (the gospel of your salvation)—when you believed in Christ—you were marked with the seal of the promised Holy Spirit. (Ephesians 1:13 NET)

That seal—the Holy Spirit—is our living, breathing divine order of protection who boldly proclaims to the Enemy, "She is *mine!* You cannot have her!"

So does that mean there is some sort of supernatural force field around us that keeps the Enemy at bay? Sometimes.

> Shadrach, Meshach, and Abednego, fell into the furnace of blazing fire while still securely bound. Then King Nebuchadnezzar was startled and quickly got up. He said to his ministers, "Wasn't it three men that we tied up and threw into the fire?" They replied to the king, "For sure, O king." He answered, "But I see four men, untied and walking around in the midst of the fire! No harm has come to them! And the appearance of the fourth is like that of a god!" … Nebuchadnezzar exclaimed, "Praised be the God of Shadrach, Meshach, and Abednego, who has sent forth his angel and has rescued his servants who trusted in him." (Daniel 3:23–25, 28 NET)

But the stories of God's deliverance *out of* Satan's clutches have to be considered alongside the stories of God's deliverance *into* suffering at the hands of Satan.

> So the LORD said to Satan, "Behold, he is in your power, only spare his life." Then Satan went out from the presence of the LORD and

smote Job with sore boils from the sole of his foot to the crown of his head. (Job 2:6–7)

Consequently, one might argue that divine orders of protection are about as trustworthy as human restraining orders. But that is shortsighted. Yes, the earthly realm is penetrable by the Enemy. But the heavenly realm is out of his reach.

> Blessed be the God and Father of our Lord Jesus Christ! By his great mercy he gave us new birth into a living hope through the resurrection of Jesus Christ from the dead, that is, into an inheritance imperishable, undefiled, and unfading. It is reserved in heaven for you. (1 Peter 1:3–4 NET)

And that hope—God's promise of eternal life with Him—should empower us in this life to stare down an assailant, or a persecutor, or an illness, or grief, or poverty, or disaster, or whatever threatens our security and say, "You don't scare me! I am His!" What extraordinary peace can be discovered when we embrace our identity in Him and His promise to never leave or forsake us.

Does that mean we should passively accept threats on our lives and well-being? Absolutely not. Life is a precious gift from God, and we should earnestly seek to protect it. But it is foolish to put our full confidence in the world when the prince of this world is on the prowl, seeking to strike terror in our hearts and minds. This world can offer some protection (though sometimes it is as flimsy as the paper it is written on), but only the Lord can offer lasting security and peace.

> Be of sober spirit, be on the alert. Your adversary, the devil, prowls around like a roaring lion, seeking someone to devour. But resist him, firm in your faith, knowing that the same experiences of suffering are being accomplished by your brethren who are in the world. After you have suffered for a little while, the God of all grace, who called you to His eternal glory in Christ, will Himself perfect, confirm, strengthen and establish you. To Him be dominion forever and ever. Amen. (1 Peter 5:8–11)

Mighty God,
This world can be such a scary place, and I hate that,
not only for me but for people I love
who are being abused by the wicked of the world.
But in Your Word, Lord, You tell us to expect trouble
in this world that is ruled by the Enemy.
Often we can't prevent trouble, and You might not stop it.
That's not because You are cruel.
You are a good and loving God who seeks our good
and Your glory, and sometimes that means
we have to come face to face with evil,
just as Your Son did.
But He claimed victory over the Enemy,
not just for His glory but for the eternal salvation
of all those who put their trust in Him.
Thank You, Father, that You have sealed
that eternal promise with the Holy Spirit.
With His empowerment, I can come face to face
with wickedness in this world, submit to the
sanctification that You achieve through my suffering,
and come out on the other side praising and glorifying You.
What man means for evil You mean for good.
Hallelujah!
In the triumphant Name of Christ Jesus, I pray.
Amen.

If He Came to Bring Peace, Why the Sword?

For some twenty years I have created a special calendar for my family. Filling it with pictures and memories from the past year and years gone by, it has always been a joy-filled project for me. As painstaking and time-consuming as it is, it is truly a labor of love. The reward comes with the laughter, smiles, and happy tears of loved ones who, with the turn of each month's page, are met with sweet family moments and cherished memories.

In recent years, however, the calendar project has not only brought delight to my heart but also a watershed of sorrow—tears of grief over fractured relationships. I had hoped that our differences could be set aside and that we could be the perfectly happy family reflected in our calendar. But that hope has drowned in my tears.

This wave of grief over family strife shouldn't have caught me by surprise. Jesus Himself struggled with His family and warned of discord.

> Do not think that I came to bring peace on the earth; I did not come to bring peace, but a sword. For I came to set a man against his father, and a daughter against her mother, and a daughter-in-law against her mother-in-law; and a man's enemies will be the members of his household. (Matthew 10:34–36)

This verse has always been puzzling to me, but never personal, until now as it echoes through my grieving heart and mind. On the surface, this passage sounds like Jesus is saying that He wants to (or even intends to)

119

divide and destroy families. But I know that is not in keeping with Scripture and with Isaiah's prophecy of the One who would be called "Wonderful Counselor, Mighty God, Eternal Father, Prince of Peace" (Isaiah 9:6). To grasp what Jesus is really saying, we need to go deeper and consider the context of the passage within its placement in the book of Matthew and within first century Judaism.

The Gospel of Matthew was originally written for Jews who had waited thousands of years for their conquering King to arrive. Since the fall in the Garden of Eden, God's people anticipated a Messiah, the "Prince of Peace" who would establish His sovereign Kingdom on earth and rule over all creation. Isaiah prophesied that it would be an earthly kingdom in which there would be "no end to the increase of His government or of peace" (Isaiah 9:7).

So generation after generation, the Israelites looked forward to the fulfillment of that promise and wondered if it would happen in their lifetime. And they had a vision of what their Messiah would look like—a mighty warrior who would rescue them from the oppression of Gentile rule. Along comes Jesus, who looked and acted more like a shepherd than a savior. And when Jesus didn't fit the Jewish image of the Messiah, the Nation of Israel rejected Him. Think about that. His own people wanted nothing to do with Him!

In Matthew 10, Jesus is preparing His twelve disciples for similar betrayal. Soon they would be going out into the world to preach, "The kingdom of heaven is at hand" (Matthew 10:7). Carrying such good news, the disciples would have reasonably expected to be received with jubilation and fanfare. But Jesus knew that it would be more like a slap in the face. The disciples would suffer greatly for their obedient service to God, not only at the hands of their countrymen, but more painfully at the hands of their own kin.

That knowledge would strike at the heart of a first century Jew whose life revolved around the family and lineage that defined him. To be cut off of from family and deleted from the family genealogy would have been unthinkable. Jesus was trying to prepare them for what was certain to be a crushing blow. Consider again the words of the self-proclaimed Jewish Messiah who was expected to usher in an everlasting Kingdom of Peace.

Do not think that I came to bring peace on the earth; I did not come to bring peace, but a sword. For I came to set a man against his father, and a daughter against her mother, and a daughter-in-law against her mother-in-law; and a man's enemies will be the members of his household. (Matthew 10:34–36)

No doubt, Jesus' words pierced the hearts of the disciples, and that was the intended result. Christ wanted them to count the cost of following Him. Obedience to Him had the potential for being an exceedingly divisive choice. But the Lord demanded nothing less than complete commitment to Him, above all other relationships.

He who loves father or mother more than Me is not worthy of Me; and he who loves son or daughter more than Me is not worthy of Me. (Matthew 10:37)

The Lord's truth is as relevant now as it was then. Christ-followers should expect rejection from those in the world who don't think the way we do, including family members. The reason for their rejection may be disguised as a disagreement, harsh words, or hurt feelings. But ultimately, rejection in a Christian's life often has spiritual roots.

My beloved mentor and pastor, the late Dr. J. Dwight Pentecost, often reminded me of a hard but important reality. We all live in one of two spheres in this world—God's realm of light and the Enemy's realm of darkness. These two spheres coexist, side by side in a world that is currently ruled by Satan, the Prince of Darkness. It is not uncommon for families to be divided—some in the light and some in the darkness. Those in the dark often hoard anger, bitterness, and unforgiveness like ammunition to be used in future battle. However in the light, we see that the war has already been won. There is no need for ammunition. We have the sword of Christ. And it is that same sword that divides a family.

Honestly, that hurt my heart. But Christ's warning is not meant to be discouraging. His warning is designed to strengthen our hearts for Him, to challenge us to put our complete, undivided trust in Him, no matter the cost.

I realize now that my grief over torn family ties has been a distraction in my relationship with the Lord. That is not acceptable to Him or to me. I won't give up on my loved ones. But I also won't give in to despair over something that Christ warned would happen. Today I have heeded his warning and counted the cost of following Him. The price is pretty high. But the One who is called "Wonderful Counselor, Mighty God, Eternal Father, Prince of Peace" deserves my undivided worship and commitment, no matter the cost.

Lord,
Teach me Your ways that I may walk in Your Truth.
Give me an undivided heart that I may fear Your name.
And I will give thanks to You,
O Lord my God, with all my heart.
I will praise Your name forever.
For Your lovingkindness toward me is great.
You have rescued my soul from Sheol.
Years ago, as I began to dive deep into Your Word,
You buried this prayer from Psalm 86
deep within my heart.
Now I understand that You did so
knowing the sorrow that would come my way.
Lord, You may not always
take us out of our struggles.
But You always enter into them,
teaching, equipping, and empowering us
to stand firm in our faith, no matter the cost.
The cost for me, and for so many others,
has been high.
But You are worth it God.
Knowing that I am, above all else, Your daughter,
brings peace that I never would have known
without the struggle.
I praise and worship You and give You thanks
in the name of Your Son, Jesus Christ,
who demonstrated His allegiance to You,
God the Father, by enduring the Cross.
It is in His faithful Name that I pray.
Amen.

R.I.P.

R.I.P. "Rest in Peace." Yep, that's what I said. Rest in Peace. And I really mean it. I pray for a R.I.P. kind of existence for all of us. No, I don't have a death wish (although the wind, snow, and ice of Wyoming may be the death of me!). What I have is an R.I.P. *life wish.*

For centuries, "Rest in Peace," a wish for the dead, has been etched on tombstones, tattooed on bodies, painted on memorials, and spoken in hushed tones at funerals. Popularized by the Roman Catholics in the eighteenth century, "Rest in Peace" comes from the Latin blessing *requiescat in pace,* which literally means "may he begin to rest in peace."

But I have come to a countercultural conclusion about that age-old adage. R.I.P. shouldn't be prayed over the dead whose eternal life has already been determined by God. R.I.P. should be prayed over the living, over those of us who are trying to live Christ-centered lives in a frantic world that promotes panic over peace.

Rest is important to the Lord, so much so that He set the example for it at the beginning of Creation.

By the seventh day God completed His work which He had done, and He rested on the seventh day from all His work which He had done. Then God blessed the seventh day and sanctified it, because in it He rested from all His work which God had created and made. (Genesis 2:2–3)

God didn't need the rest. After all, He's God! But He took that seventh day to simply enjoy His Creation, His glory. He wants the same for His people. Resting on the seventh day is not about taking a break from work. It's about taking time with God. From Genesis through Revelation, God promotes, and even commands, rest among His people, for our enjoyment as well as His.

> For six days work may be done, but on the seventh day there is a Sabbath of complete rest, holy to the LORD. (Exodus 31:15)

Easier said than done, you may be saying, as you rush to school to pick up the kids and get them to all of their after-school activities, as traffic threatens to push your nervous system over the edge, as the pressures of work and providing for your family mount, as the bills from the holiday season are starting to come in and Uncle Sam is also holding out his hand, and as the cat is screaming for his food which you forgot to pick up. *Whew!* Who has time to *rest* in all of this dizzying chaos?!

You do.

Do you really think your Creator—the God who hung the moon and the stars; the God who gave shape, size, color, and purpose to every flower you see; the God who is familiar with every hair on your head (most of all the gray ones!)—do you really think He can't help you carve out a little time in your busy schedule to just rest and be with Him? And have you stopped long enough to consider what a waste of time it is to bow to the tyranny of the urgent rather than the Prince of Peace?

> Unless the LORD builds the house,
> They labor in vain who build it;
> Unless the LORD guards the city,
> The watchman keeps awake in vain.
> It is vain for you to rise up early,
> To retire late,
> To eat the bread of painful labors;
> For He gives to His beloved even in his sleep. (Psalm 127:1–2)

You might want to give it a shot and just ask Him. That alone requires you to pause in your day and turn your attention toward Him. But believer beware, once you start resting in Him, you are bound to experience peace that you never have before. And He just might become more important to you than your daily chaos. Let it be so, Lord, let it be so.

God of rest and peace,
How did we get to this place
where things are so chaotic and upside down
that our time to rest in You
has taken a backseat to carpools and traffic?
It's baffling to me that I would choose
my to-do list over my Creator, and yet I do.
Forgive me, Lord, for not putting You first.
You want me to spend time with You,
not because You need the rest,
but because I need the rest and peace
that comes only in the quiet moments
of communing with my Savior.
Lord, I offer You my willing heart.
Would You help me carve out time in the day
to rest in You?
It is in the Name of Jesus Christ,
the Prince of Peace, that I offer this request.
Amen.

CHAPTER 8

Basement
Reflections
on
*Praising
the Lord*

My Liver Sings!

Did You Hear What Mary Said?

Now That's an Amazing *Feet*!

Go Gold! Go, God!

My Liver Sings!

"In the two years I have been doing this, no one has ever said anything like that to me," the young man named Pas muttered in a tone that fell somewhere between skepticism and curiosity. After spending numerous frustrating hours over several days on the phone with me trying to fix my computer, the last thing Pas expected to hear from me was, "How can I pray for you?" (especially because he could not immediately resolve my technology issues).

To be honest, it was the last thing I wanted to do. I didn't want to follow the Lord's leading to pray for Pas. I just wanted to get off the phone and pout. But just before Pas hung up, I did what the Lord asked. And in the middle of the night, at a crowded call center on another continent, a gentle soul sat dumbfounded, almost speechless. But it wasn't a broken computer that stumped him. It was the Lord. In joyful disbelief Pas said, "You can pray for good health and success for me and that I will get another customer like you in the New Year, someone who would also be kind and willing to pray for me."

At that moment, my liver sang!

It's true! My "liver" sang! (And it had nothing to do with all the southern fried food I consumed on my vacation in Pigeon Forge, Tennessee, where Dolly Parton and butter are hometown heroes).

A "singing liver" was an idiom used by the writers of the Psalms to express joy found in the Lord and His redemption.

Then you turned my lament into dancing;

you removed my sackcloth and covered me with joy.
So now my heart [liver] will sing to you and not be silent;
O Lord my God, I will always give thanks to you.
(Psalm 30:11–12 NET)

Like the heart, the liver was viewed by our spiritual ancestors as the seat of one's emotions. Modern Bible translators don't use *liver* for obvious cultural reasons. (Imagine getting a liver-shaped box of chocolates on Valentine's Day!) But in the original Hebrew Scriptures, joy in the Lord is sourced in a grateful liver.

My heart [liver] is steadfast, O God, my heart [liver] is steadfast;
I will sing, yes, I will sing praises!
Awake, my glory!
Awake, harp and lyre!
I will awaken the dawn.
I will give thanks to You, O Lord, among the peoples;
I will sing praises to You among the nations.
For Your lovingkindness is great to the heavens
And Your truth to the clouds. (Psalm 57:7–10)

I have to say, I prefer the "liver" translation. One of the hardest working organs in the body, it was created by God to filter what we eat and drink, to separate the good from the bad, the nutritional from the toxic. I don't know if the ancients understood the physiological function of the liver. But it is clear that they understood its spiritual function, its role in removing emotional toxins and fueling worship for and joy in the Lord.

What a workout my spiritual liver has been getting lately! One day I consume extra helpings of love. The next day I sit down to a plate full of grief, loneliness, and family strife. In fact, today I woke up with an extra helping of hurt sticking to my ribs. My spiritual liver was working overtime to manage the toxins of disappointment and depression. But in a moment that caught me by surprise as much as it did my new friend Pas, my liver sang! Why? The second I followed the Lord's lead to offer some Christian love to Pas, my heart (liver) swelled with joy.

I have set the Lord continually before me;

Because He is at my right hand, I will not be shaken.
Therefore my heart is glad and my glory [liver] rejoices;
My flesh also will dwell securely. (Psalm 16:8–9)

And joy, like chocolate, should be in a food category of its own! Like chocolate, joy seems to taste even sweeter when it comes as an unexpected surprise. And also like chocolate, joy is addictive. Once you've tasted it, you can't get enough of it.

Forrest Gump famously said, "Life is a box of chocolates. You never know what you're gonna get."[1] I think that's true. You never know what or who the Lord is going to put in your path. But you do know how He wants you to react—with love. And when you are obedient to that calling, joy will fill your heart and song will break out in your liver!

Oh God, how I love You!
I love that You love to challenge and surprise me.
And I am so grateful that in that once-in-a-lifetime
moment with Pas, I followed Your lead.
I can still hear my liver singing!
Precious Father, I earnestly pray that You
put more obedient Christ-followers in his path
and that You have drawn him close
through the kindness and love of others.
And I pray that this little story of obedience
will encourage others to take a little extra time
to love on the strangers
who we call on every day to serve us.
The dishwasher repair man, the kid flipping burgers,
the cashier at the convenience store, the postal clerk,
and yes, even the police officer running the speed trap.
You love them and we should too.
When we do, an entire chorus of livers will sing!
To God be the glory forever and ever.
Amen.

Did You Hear What Mary Said?

And Mary said, "Behold, the bondslave of the Lord; may it be done to me according to your word." (Luke 1:38)

Did you hear what Mary just said? "May it be done to me according to your word." Incredible! How was she able to so willingly and joyfully (Luke 1:46) respond to the news from the angel Gabriel?

We might be quick to say, "What's so surprising? Who wouldn't want to bring the long-awaited Messiah into the world?" But put yourself in Mary's shoes, and you might think again.

In her time, centuries ago, young Jewish girls were married in their early-to-mid teens. We know from Scripture that Mary was betrothed or engaged to Joseph, so it is likely she was around fourteen, fifteen, maybe sixteen years old. She was just a girl, a girl in a culture where virginity was a life or death issue. A young bride found impure before her wedding night could be divorced by her husband and stoned to death by her community. Did you get that? The penalty for impurity of a young, betrothed girl back then was *death*—in the gruesome and painful manner of stoning!

Pause for a moment and let that settle in. Imagine the life-changing and potentially life-ending enormity of that moment of truth: Mary, you are about to be a pregnant, unwed teenager in a world where girls who are not virgins at the time of their wedding can be stoned to death.

What would you do? How would you respond?

Have you heard what Mary said? "May it be done to me according to your word." Then later in the first chapter of Luke, we read how Mary, now pregnant, unwed, and visiting relatives, offers up one of the most exquisite praise songs ever sung to the Lord, the song we today call the Magnificat, recorded in Luke 1:46–55. Mary begins with:

> My soul exalts the Lord,
> And my spirit has rejoiced in God my Savior.
> For He has had regard for the humble state of His bondslave;
> For behold, from this time on all generations will count me blessed.
> For the Mighty One has done great things for me;
> And holy is His name. (Luke 1:46–49)

Blessed? A great thing? To be pregnant before she is wed? Not only did she welcome the news from the angel, but she rejoiced in it and praised God for it! The natural human response would not be praise. It would be panic! We have plenty of biblical examples of that. When the Lord gave the charge to Moses to lead the Israelites out of Egypt, Moses claimed a speech impediment disqualified him for the job. When the Lord told Jonah to go to the wicked town of Nineveh and preach repentance, Jonah ran away from home! When Peter—one of Jesus' beloved disciples—was asked to declare his allegiance to the Lord, three times he denied Jesus out of fear for his own skin! Panic was a natural response back then. And let's be honest, it is the default response for most of us now. When the Lord asks us to do something or endure something that is not in our game plan, it's game over.

Fear, panic, denial, escape. That's just what we do.

So how was Mary, just a young teen, able to respond in praise? She *knew* God. She *believed* God. And she *anticipated* God.

Mary *knew* God. How does one know God? By diligently studying His Word which reveals His Character. Mary knew the Scriptures so well that they were imbedded in her consciousness, in her every thought. This brave, young teenager was a true student of the Scriptures. We know this, because at the most terrifying moment of her young life, the Song of Hannah recorded in 1 Samuel 2:1–10, was front and center in her thoughts.

Hannah was praising God for opening her barren womb and giving her a son, Samuel. See if it sounds familiar. It should. The echo of Hannah's song hundreds of years before rang in Mary's head and heart as she sang out to the Lord.

Hannah's song (1 Samuel 2:1–10)	Mary's song (Luke 1:46–55)
My heart exults in the LORD; My horn is exalted in the LORD, ... I rejoice in Your salvation. (verse 1)	My soul exalts the Lord, And my spirit has rejoiced in God my Savior. (verses 46–47)
There is no one holy like the LORD, Indeed, there is no one besides You. (verse 2)	For the Mighty One has done great things for me; And holy is His name. (verse 49)
The bows of the mighty are shattered, But the feeble gird on strength." (verse 4)	He has brought down rulers from their thrones, And has exalted those who were humble. (verse 52)
Those who were full hire themselves out for bread, But those who were hungry cease to hunger. (verse 5)	He has filled the hungry with good things; And sent away the rich empty-handed. (verse 53)

Their songs are not identical. Mary's is uniquely hers. But it echoes the truths about God that she learned from Hannah and the rest of the Scriptures. Mary is a student of the Word. And through the Word, she has come to know God and His Character. The truth about God and His Word is in the front of her mind all the time.

Mary also *believed* God. This young teen had placed her trust in the Lord. She believed to her very core that God would be faithful to her, that He would never abandon or forsake her. She knew this from His track record with her ancestors. He parted the Red Sea for the Israelites and rescued them from the iron-fisted grip of Pharaoh and the Egyptians. He provided water and food for His people in the wilderness—the desert where food and water didn't exist and no one can survive without divine intervention. And He brought Mary's people into the Promised Land, just as He had promised. Mary looked to the past and saw the Lord as a Promise Keeper and a Deliverer, and she believed that He would deliver on what He promised her—a child who would one day become King and reign over His people forever. Despite what the world might think and how her community might respond to her growing belly, Mary put her trust in God. She believed!

Finally, Mary *anticipated* God. From the fall in the Garden of Eden down through the centuries, the Lord had time and again promised that He would send a Messiah to His people, a Savior, a "Wonderful Counselor," a "Prince of Peace," who, according to the prophet Isaiah, would be born of a virgin and would rescue His people from the oppression of evil. From generation to generation, the Israelites waited for this promised Messiah. Meanwhile, the disobedience of the nation of Israel became so intolerable that God went silent on them. For four hundred years not a single Jew heard from the Lord.

Four hundred years is the gap of time between the end of the Old Testament and the beginning of the New Testament, where we meet Mary, a young, God-fearing Jewish girl who had hope. She knew her God to be trustworthy, a Promise Keeper. And she believed God's promise that He would send a Savior. So she anticipated the Messiah's arrival—even in her own lifetime—and she lived her life accordingly.

When the angel Gabriel appeared to her, was she surprised? Sure! But she had steeped herself in Scripture, placed her trust in the Lord, and maintained a constant watch for her Savior. He arrived—in her own womb! There was not panic; there was praise. She said, "My soul exalts the Lord."

Even as a teenage girl, she got it—the profound understanding that God is sovereign. He either causes or allows all circumstances in our lives, even those that we think could destroy us. And He does so for His glory and our good. He is worthy of our praise, no matter our circumstances.

After the most excruciating season of my life, I finally get it too, at the very core of my being. At the beginning of my struggles, my response was fear and panic. But through a gut-wrenchingly painful season, God has demonstrated His faithfulness, so much so that I can praise Him, even though He has yet to deliver me from my tribulation.

I *know* God. He is sovereign and good. I *believe* that He is trustworthy with His promises. And I *anticipate* Him in all circumstances.

What about you? When that unforeseen challenge comes your way—illness, loss, betrayal, broken relationships, professional failure, financial disaster—will you panic or praise God in the midst of your struggle?

Lord,
You have proven Yourself faithful and trustworthy,
from the cradle to the Cross.
You, and You alone,
are worthy of our praise and worship.
But too often we choose panic over praise.
When life gets hard,
we should get on our knees and give thanks,
knowing that You will faithfully see us through the trial.
Instead, we get on our knees and beg You to make it stop.
Countless nights I have pleaded with You
to just bring me Home so I would no longer
have to suffer and struggle.
And every morning following my plea
You breathed life into my lungs.
I get it now.
While You didn't take me out of my suffering,
You entered into my suffering to teach me who You are,
a faithful, trustworthy, loving Father
who wants only what is best for His child,
even when "best" feels really bad.
Thank You, Lord. My soul exalts You.
In the Name of My Savior, Jesus Christ.
Amen.

Now That's an Amazing *Feet*!

How 'bout those Villanova Wildcats! Unbelievable! Shocking!! Astonishing!!! And *then,* they went out and won the 2016 NCAA National Basketball Championship.

Oh, did you think I was describing that crazy three-pointer made with less than a second left in the game? That was pretty cool too. But I'm talking about what you would have witnessed had you been in the locker room just before Villanova's Sweet 16 victory on March 24, 2016. You would have seen the Wildcats washing each other's feet. How I wish there was a replay on that!

It was Maundy Thursday. The team was gearing up for their game against Miami when Villanova's Associate Athletic Director and Chaplain, Robert Hagan, asked each member of the team—everyone from starters to walk-ons—to wash another player's feet.

> He got up from the meal, removed his outer clothes, took a towel and tied it around himself. He poured water into the washbasin and began to wash the disciples' feet and to dry them with the towel He had wrapped around himself. (John 13:4–5 NET)

Two thousand years ago, if you had been a first century Jewish "fly on the wall" in that upper room, you would have thought you were hallucinating (even more than seeing twenty-first century basketball players take a cue from Jesus!). The rabbi, teacher, revolutionary, self-proclaimed Son of God was kneeling to wash the feet of cultural outcasts? MIND-BLOWING!

In those days people wore sandals. There were no paved roads or sidewalks, so folks' feet got dirty. *Really* dirty. It was customary for a host to order a servant to wash his guests' feet. The task was so degrading that even Hebrew slaves were spared the humiliation of cleansing filthy, stinky feet.

Yet Jesus took it upon Himself.

So when Jesus had washed their feet and put his outer clothing back on, he took his place at the table again and said to them, "Do you understand what I have done for you? You call me 'Teacher' and 'Lord,' and do so correctly, for that is what I am. If I then, your Lord and Teacher, have washed your feet, you too ought to wash one another's feet. ... I tell you the solemn truth, the slave is not greater than his master, nor is the one who is sent as a messenger greater than the one who sent him. If you understand these things, you will be blessed if you do them." (John 13:12–14, 16–17 NET)

"If you understand these things, you will be blessed if you do them." Can you imagine the looks of bewilderment on the faces of the disciples? I'm guessing most of those Villanova basketball players were similarly perplexed. But, wow, were they blessed!

After humbling themselves to wash each other's feet (fungus or no fungus), they crushed their opponent in the Sweet 16 game and went on to win the NCAA Championship. Now, I wouldn't presume that God gave them the victory as some sort of spiritual reward. This is not a lesson on prosperity gospel. But I am certain that those young men learned a little something about humility and selflessness, and it showed on the court.

Villanova senior Ryan Arcidiacono had dreamed all of his life about being the guy who got the game-winning basket at the buzzer.

"With 4.7 seconds left on the clock and the score tied at 74, he had the ball and headed toward the basket. He dribbled up the court thinking, 'I'm going to shoot this!' Then, he took the ball— and passed it? ... When Arcidiacono heard his teammate Kris Jenkins shouting, 'Arch! Arch!' because he was open, Arcidiacono turned and tossed the ball to him. That single flick of the ball set up one of the most stunning moments in N.C.A.A. tournament history. Jenkins let the ball fly, and it seemed that the nearly 75,000 spectators dropped their jaws and hushed their breath in unison. As the horn blared, the ball slid through the hoop to score 3 points, and the entire stadium roared … 'Arch was supposed to shoot it because he's a senior and that's what seniors do when the final game's on the line,' Jenkins said. 'But he gave it to me, and I really can't believe it. It just shows what kind of person he is.'"[2]

Selflessness. It's a rare quality in today's world, so rare that it causes jaws to drop. Most of us will never cause 75,000 jaws to drop with one act of selflessness. But would you trade 75,000 high-fives for one soul? I would!

For the Christ-follower, selflessness is an act of praise and worship. We honor and glorify our Savior when we put others first.

Do nothing from selfishness or empty conceit, but with humility of mind regard one another as more important than yourselves; do not merely look out for your own personal interests, but also for the interests of others. Have this attitude in yourselves which was also in Christ Jesus. (Philippians 2:3–5)

There are boundless opportunities today for each of us to praise the Lord by having the mind of Christ. It may be as simple as giving up your prime airplane seat to someone behind you who is uncomfortably stuck in a middle. Or sacrificing victory to team up with the kid who is always picked last. Have you ever thought of surrendering a cherished Saturday to babysit (for free!) for a single mom who never gets a day off? What about offering one of your valuable vacation days to a colleague in need of more sick leave? You probably won't make the headlines for your selflessness. But you will make an impression. When folks ask why, tell them about Jesus, our Lord who loves them so much that he would do something even more shocking. He would wash their stinky feet!

If you know these things, you are blessed if you do them. (John 13:17)

Father God,
Humility is at the heart of who You are.
Jesus began and ended His life on earth
with the two greatest acts of selflessness of all time.
The King of Kings stepped out of Heaven,
veiled His glory behind human flesh,
and arrived on earth via a birth canal.
Some thirty-three years later,
He submitted to death on the Cross
while the people He came to save
cursed and spit at him.
How could I not want to be humble and selfless
given what He did for me?
And yet, much of the time I don't think of others first.
I'm mostly concerned with myself and what I want.
By Your Spirit, will You open my eyes
to opportunities today to live out the humility
and selflessness of Christ?
Surprise me. Challenge me.
And when I'm asked, "Why did you do that?"
give me the courage and the words
to tell them about Jesus.
In His Name and for His glory and honor, I pray.
Amen.

Go Gold! Go, God!

"We both know that our identity is in Christ," David Boudia said matter-of-factly.[3]

Whaaaaat?! Did I just hear what I think I heard? An Olympic silver medalist giving glory to Christ on live television?

"The fact that I was going into this event knowing that my identity is rooted in Christ and not what the result of this competition is just gave me peace," added Boudia's diving partner, Steele Johnson.

"Wow! We're just getting started and already these are the best Olympics ever!" I thought out loud. The way David Boudia and Steele Johnson twisted and flipped their way to Olympic silver in synchronized diving was awe-inspiring in and of itself. But it was how they turned the diving platform into a platform for the Lord that took my breath away.

And then, on NBC's TODAY show, gymnastics phenom Simone Biles gave glory to the Lord for her talent and collection of medals (mostly gold).

And then, just minutes after winning the 400 meter in record-setting time, South African runner Wayde van Niekerk credited the Lord for his gold medal. "The only thing I can do now is to give God praise," he told the media.[4]

But also, Christ's name was lifted up in the agony of defeat. The 100-meter hopeful Trayvon Bromell tweeted this after missing out on a medal: "People telling me to hold my head up...do y'all not know the God we serve, I will never hold my head down. God is great! #Blessed."[5]

Can I get an *amen*? And did you happen to see the awful crash in the 5,000-meter qualifying heat? Runners Abbey D'Agostino and Nikki

Hamblin both went down. D'Agostino helped her rival to her feet. And the two of them helped one another finish the race. The world called it impressive sportsmanship. Abbey D'Agostino called it Christ. "Although my actions were instinctual at the moment, the only way I can and have rationalized it is that God prepared my heart to respond that way. This whole time here he's made clear to me that my experience in Rio was going to be about more than my race performance – and as soon as Nikki got up I knew that was it."[6]

Unbelievable! Jesus Christ taking one victory lap after another on the world's largest stage. How ironic given that the Olympic Games originated as part of a religious festival honoring the Greek god Zeus, king of the Greek pantheon. The Olympics was (and one could argue still is) a festival celebrating false deities and elevating men to almost god-like status. An absolute affront to the Lord. And yet, we see Olympic imagery throughout the New Testament.

> We must get rid of every weight and the sin that clings so closely, and run with endurance the race set out for us, keeping our eyes fixed on Jesus, the pioneer and perfecter of our faith. For the joy set out for him he endured the cross, disregarding its shame, and has taken his seat at the right hand of the throne of God. Think of him who endured such opposition against himself by sinners, so that you may not grow weary in your souls and give up. (Hebrews 12:1–3 NET)

Why on earth would the New Testament writers, who were teaching new believers how to reject the world and obediently follow Jesus Christ, go anywhere near pagan culture in their writings? Because that's where the first century believers lived, smack-dab in the middle of pagan culture. In His brilliance God connects with what is culturally relevant at the time and then in perfect form turns culture on its head.

> Run in such a way that you may win. Everyone who competes in the games exercises self-control in all things. They then do it to receive a perishable wreath, but we an imperishable. (1 Corinthians 9:24–25)

In Paul's day an Olympic champion didn't receive a medal. He was crowned with a wreath made from the branches of a wild olive tree. The "laurel wreath" celebrated the ultimate in human accomplishment and made the victor an instant hero. It must have been something to behold! Until it withered and died.

The life of a Christ-follower looks a lot like an elite athlete, requiring commitment, focus, sacrifice, tenacity, and strength-training. But when all is said and done, the Christian's reward far outruns that of the Olympian. When the Christian crosses his finish line, he will be crowned with a victor's wreath that will never wither and die. Now that's solid gold!

And speaking of gold, did you get a look at Usain Bolt's running shoes? Guess who he credits for bringing those shiny shoes across the finish line in record time? Go, God! Go gold!

Oh God,
How fun it is to see You show up in places
where we wouldn't expect You.
You never cease to amaze me
at how You can take something
intended to glorify man and flip-flop it into
honor and glory for You.
You and You alone are worthy of
our praise and adoration.
Not even the greatest athletes, or rock stars,
or Hollywood celebrities, or world leaders
could speak Creation into existence
or raise themselves from the dead.
Thank You that there are folks who,
when You give them the platform,
will lift up Your Name and not their own.
Your Name is above all names, and one day,
every knee will bow at Your Name.
What a day that will be!
Even better than the Olympics!
I love you, God.
In Your Son's magnificent Name, I pray.
Amen.

CHAPTER 9

Basement Reflections
on
Trusting the Lord

Cross to Bear

The Lord is My Shepherd

Yoked

Shalom

Cross to Bear

"Is this my cross to bear?" my friend asked, her voice shrinking with the concession that her life would forevermore stagnate in pain, sorrow, and regret. I thought to myself, *Is it Lord? Is this her cross to bear? What exactly is a "cross to bear"?*

I have heard (and said) the expression more times than I can count. Often it is used to solicit compassion or pity.

Like chronic illness. "Cancer is his cross to bear."

Sometimes it's used in jest.

Like bad hair. "Frizz is my cross to bear."

And sometimes it's used in just plain absurdity.

"*The Exorcist* has been a very interesting cross to bear," said Linda Blair, the head-spinning child star from the 1973 horror flick *The Exorcist*.[1] (True quote. You can't make this stuff up!)

The world views a "cross to bear" as an unavoidable burden or trial. Alzheimer's is a cross to bear for the whole family. Someone has to mow the lawn. It's my weekly cross to bear.

Isn't that just like the world and the Prince of Darkness to take the words of Jesus and twist them for their own self-serving use? Let's take a look at the biblical text from which the world draws its cheap, knock-off cross to bear.

In Matthew 16, Peter proclaims Jesus is the Christ (verse 16). But as Jesus is teaching His disciples that He must die, Peter rebukes Him. That drew a fiery response from the Lord.

He turned and said to Peter, "Get behind Me, Satan! You are a stumbling block to Me; for you are not setting your mind on God's interests, but man's." Then Jesus said to His disciples, "If anyone wishes to come after Me, let him deny himself, and take up his cross and follow Me." (Matthew 16:23–24)

Who could blame Peter? He didn't want the Messiah to die. But Jesus is clear: It's not about you, Peter. And what's more, by demanding your own will rather than the Lord's, you are doing exactly what Satan wants you to do, become a stumbling block to God's will in this world.

Turn to Luke 14, where Jesus offers a parable about a dinner party. When the host is ready and the table is set, none of the guests show up. Everyone has an excuse for their absence. One man has new property needing his attention. Another has new oxen needing to be trained. A third man says his wife is waiting for him. All of them put their own personal interests and desires ahead of their host's hospitality. The moral of Jesus' story:

If anyone comes to Me, and does not hate his own father and mother and wife and children and brothers and sisters, yes, and even his own life, he cannot be My disciple. Whoever does not carry his own cross and come after Me cannot be My disciple. (Luke 14:26–27)

Do you find that hard to swallow? I do! And that's *exactly* what the Enemy is counting on—us allowing our personal relationships, interests, desires, and failures to distract us from following God's will.

It is important to clarify the meaning of three key words spoken by Jesus in the above passage.

- *Hate.* The Greek word here refers to human will, not emotion. "To hate is to refuse to submit to the authority of another," explains Dr. Dwight Pentecost.[2]
- *Disciple.* Within the context, *disciple* is not simply one who believes in Christ. A "disciple" is one who submits his will to the will of God.

- *Cross.* In Jesus' metaphor, *cross* represents obedience to God. It's not the thing you are giving up for the Lord. Your "cross" is your act of obedience to the Lord no matter the cost.

The actual wooden cross on which Jesus was crucified is believed to have weighed about 300 pounds, beyond brutal for any human to carry on a scourged and bloodied back. But the physical weight of that cross was like a feather on Jesus' back compared to our sin. Yet, out of obedience to the Father, Jesus carried it even though the mere thought of it made Him sweat blood.

Recall that in the Garden of Gethsemane, Jesus asked the Father to let this horrific cup (this cross to bear) pass from Him. It wasn't the thought of the physical pain that created those bloody beads of sweat. It was the reality that, for the first time in all of eternity, the Son would be spiritually separated from the Father. As He became sin for us and paid our sin debt of death, the consequence for Him would be physical and spiritual separation from the Father (the penalty that we deserved, not Him). It was not something that Jesus was eager to do. But do you remember how He finished that prayer in Gethsemane? "Not my will, but Yours be done" (Luke 22:42). Jesus trusted that His Father, a good and loving Father, wouldn't ask His beloved Son to surrender to crucifixion unless it accomplished His perfect purpose and will.

If we want to be like Him, if we want to be more than believers in Christ but actual "disciples" of Christ—Christ-followers—then by His example, our "cross to bear" is obedience to God, *at all costs.*

Envision yourself on the journey to Calvary, following the Lord and carrying your cross of obedience. From the side of the road you hear your spouse or your child shout, "Am I not more important to you than Him?" Do you put down your cross to rush to their side? Others in the crowd shout: "You're going to lose your job if you keep this up!" or "People are starting to talk!" or "It's not fair that you have cancer and still have to follow Him!" or "Come on, you can't stop for just one more drink or one more peek at porn?!"

The Enemy will elevate the voice of whomever or whatever it is that we desire or value more than Christ—family, job, reputation, money, addiction—whatever it is that can distract us from putting Him first in our lives. God isn't asking us to pretend that personal relationships, passions, and pain don't exist and tug on our hearts. But He wants us to keep them in right perspective, not allowing them to take His preeminent place in our lives. That's tough to do. But it wasn't easy for Jesus, so why would it be easy for us? When that cross of obedience seems too heavy to bear, God's Word tells us what to do—take our eyes off of the price and place them squarely on the prize.

> Fixing our eyes on Jesus, the author and perfecter of faith, who for the joy set before Him endured the cross. (Hebrews 12:2)

If that seems impossible, take courage in knowing He's been exactly where you are, and He wants to help! Jesus called on supernatural strength to endure the Cross. That strength that raised Him from the dead is also available to help us in our seasons of suffering.

> But if the Spirit of Him who raised Jesus from the dead dwells in you, He who raised Christ Jesus from the dead will also give life to your mortal bodies through His Spirit who dwells in you. (Romans 8:11)

Do you believe that? I mean to the very marrow of your bones, do you believe that you have that kind of strength within you? When we wrap our brains and faith around that—the power of the resurrection resides in us—then no "cross to bear" is too heavy. Not for Jesus Christ and not for those of us who have fixed our eyes on Him.

Mighty and Merciful God,
In the midst of despair and darkness,
can I trust You over the circumstances?
I didn't know the answer to that question
until I found myself wanting to die rather than endure
another painful minute on this planet.
In that deep, dark hole of despair
I learned two valuable truths.
You are trustworthy.
And pain has purpose.

O Lord, thank You that my suffering has not been in vain!
I don't ever want to have to go through
such grief and sorrow again, God.
But if You allow future trials in my life,
I pray that I will look at the Cross and remember:
You are trustworthy.
And pain has purpose.
By Your Spirit, give me the strength to carry
whatever cross You ask me to bear.
In the Name of the One who not only
carried His Cross, but died on it—for me.
Amen.

The Lord is My Shepherd

"The Lord is my Shepherd, I shall not want." Where do those beloved words of the Bible take you? To the graveside of a loved one? To the deathbed of a friend? Without question, the Lord has used Psalm 23 to take the suffering and grieving by the hand and guide them through the valley of death. But when I read Psalm 23, the Lord takes me by the hand and leads me to a different place, a place of abundant life!

Abundant life, not death. Living in hope and confidence is what King David sings about in Psalm 23. It's a song of confidence and trust in the Lord as he views life through the youthful eyes of a shepherd boy and the weathered eyes of a warrior king.

He makes me lie down in green pastures. (Psalm 23:2a)

When David sees green pastures, he's not envisioning a well-groomed cemetery. He sees a rich blanket of grass, made fresh with a gentle rain that is more than enough to nourish a flock of sheep. Behind this imagery David sees God's Word and how it offers exceedingly abundant nourishment for the Lord's flock.

He leads me beside quiet waters. (verse 2b)

When David sees quiet waters, he's not thinking about the slow drip of an IV tube in a hospice unit. He is recalling the refreshment that he, as a young shepherd, was able to offer to his thirsty and dusty sheep, quiet waters that quenched their thirst and cleansed their bodies. The imagery of water that David paints represents the spiritual refreshment God offers through His mercy, forgiveness, and provision.

> You prepare a table before me in the presence
> of my enemies. (verse 5a)

When the Lord lays out a feast for David in the presence of his enemies, it is not a table covered with funeral food. The Lord is inviting David to experience His fellowship and provision. It's important for us to see that God doesn't take David, His chosen warrior king, out of the world to commune with Him. Rather, the Lord enters into David's world —a world occupied by real life enemies—to fellowship with and provide for his servant. This is the imagery of a faithful and trustworthy God who may not take us out of our tribulation, but instead enters into it and communes with us, right where we are.

> You have anointed my head with oil;
> My cup overflows. (verse 5b)

When the Lord anoints David's head with oil and offers him a cup that never runs dry, it is not in preparation for David's death. It is in celebration of David's life, a life distinguished by constant communion with *Yahweh*, who promises to never abandon or forsake His beloved child. This imagery recalls hospitality in the Ancient Near East where a host allowed his guests' cups to run dry only when he wanted them to leave. With God, our Host of Abundant Life, our cups will never run dry.

> Surely goodness and lovingkindness
> will follow me all the days of my life,
> And I will dwell in the house of the LORD forever. (verse 6)

In these closing words King David speaks of the trust He has in the Lord. That he will never have to live outside of God's presence, not on earth and not in eternity. Those words didn't come easily to David. At times his life seemed to reflect anything but abundance. Hunted, embattled, betrayed, deceived, tested, and tried, David's life, as evidenced in Psalms

13 and 51, was no bed of roses. But through his suffering David came to trust wholly and completely in God's loyal love.

Psalm 23 is David's *life song*! Under the inspiration of the Spirit, he composed the world's most beloved psalm in *celebration* of abundant life in the Lord.

Should it not be our *life song* too? David's God is our God. The same God who set a table for him in the presence of his enemies sets a beautiful table for us today, in this world, in the presence of the Prince of Darkness. The Lord enters into our world to commune with us, provide for us, and protect us, just as He did for David. That is definitely something to sing about!

The next time you hear Psalm 23 recited at a funeral, grieve for the dead and those who are left behind. But when you depart from the service, praise God, and rejoice in the green-pasture, quiet-water, cup-overflowing, abundant life that only He can provide on this side of Heaven.

Gracious and Loving Father,
You are a God of abundance!
Abundant provision, abundant love,
abundant grace, abundant fellowship,
abundant life!
By Your Spirit, help me to embrace
that extraordinary truth while I am living,
not just as I am dying.
Thank You for Your Word and for its deep teaching
that takes us beyond the basics of our faith
into a never-ending odyssey
of exploring Your Character and Truth.
That odyssey is meant to be enjoyed
with every breath we take.
Oh Lord,
my cup overflows with gratitude for the privilege
and joy of living with You every day.
You are trustworthy and faithful.
And I praise and worship You, my Living God.
In the life-giving Name of Jesus Christ.
Amen.

Yoked

It was truly an extraordinary thing to behold. Less than twenty-four hours after a rage-filled young man murdered nine people at a Bible study in Charleston, South Carolina, family members of the victims faced off with the gunman, not to condemn him but to offer their forgiveness.

Did anyone else but me say, *How do you do that?* It's not that I doubt their authenticity. I just really want to know *how* they came to that place of forgiveness so quickly when I have wrestled with it for years. In fact, if you could peer inside my heart today, you would immediately find the unforgiveness that resides there, squatting on precious real estate that belongs to God.

Forgiveness. I know that it can be done, because the Lord forgave me. And I know that it is a seemingly simple matter of trusting the Lord, placing my unforgiveness at the foot of the Cross, and leaving it there. But the path from head knowledge to heart knowledge can be a *long* journey! And while many have told me that I must forgive (just as I have told others), it's the *how* that gets lost on me in the deepest recesses of my heart, where the pain deposited by people I trusted and loved holds on with a death grip.

> Let all bitterness and wrath and anger and clamor and slander be put away from you, along with all malice. Be kind to one another, tender-hearted, forgiving each other, just as God in Christ also has forgiven you. (Ephesians 4:31–32)

Lord, I try to place my unforgiveness at the foot of the Cross, but I can't help but pick it back up when I am reminded of the betrayal, I recently prayed. *How do I leave it there and authentically (by word and heart) move from the bondage of bitterness to the freedom found in forgiveness?*

His response:

> Come to Me, all who are weary and heavy-laden, and I will give you rest. Take My yoke upon you and learn from Me, for I am gentle and humble in heart, and you will find rest for your souls. For My yoke is easy and My burden is light. (Matthew 11:28–30)

I have long thought that this passage is an offer of comfort in the midst of suffering. Certainly there is validity in that interpretation. This Scripture has comforted me in all sorts of challenging circumstances. But there is deeper truth below the surface, where I find the answer to my question, "How do I authentically forgive the very people who put me in this season of heartache?"

A *yoke* is a wooden crosspiece that binds two oxen together. Farmers in Jesus' time (and even today) would yoke a young, wild ox to a mature, trained ox in order to transform the younger animal into an effective worker for the harvest. Under a yoke, the apprentice animal and his mentor master were kept side by side, forcing the young ox into a position of restraint and submission. The immature animal, who was accustomed to going his own way, would struggle against the yoke at first. But the larger, stronger ox would respond by pulling his young companion back on the right course. In time, and with a lot of practice, the young apprentice would learn the ways of his mentor master, ultimately becoming just like him.

When Jesus first offered His yoke, He did so to Jews who were living under an oppressive religious regime. The religious elite of Israel had twisted the Law into a weapon of oppression that they used against the masses. With absolute contempt for the nation's leaders, Jesus looked past them and directly into the eyes of the people with this invitation: "Come to Me, all who are weary and heavy-laden, and I will give you rest. ... My yoke is easy and My burden is light."

Jesus invites them and us today to submit to His trustworthy authority, to yoke ourselves with Him and learn from Him how to live in true freedom. *Learn*, not magically become perfect overnight.

For me, the learning curve is steep, and the journey to forgive is long. But this passage helps me to see how I can get there. I have to trust God with my entire being, yoking myself to Him, day after day after day. There will be days when I want to veer off and do my own thing, like refusing to forgive. But if I trust the Lord to teach me, and I am solidly yoked to Him, He will always pull me back into line.

I hope that one day I will be like the rock-star oxen I admire who forgive freely and instantly. But now I realize that is a *learned* spiritual skill, and I am a young ox in training. The good news is that while I am in training and learning, I don't have to grow weary under the burden of my sin. Christ took care of that on a wooden crosspiece some two-thousand years ago, the same wooden crosspiece that now yokes me to Him.

Merciful and Forgiving God,
Oh how I would love to be able to come before You
with a pure heart, cleansed of all unforgiveness.
But I can't, and there is no sense in pretending,
because You can see my heart wounds
that ooze with bitterness and anger.
Lord, I want those wounds healed,
and I trust in You, the Great Physician,
to make that happen.
But I also understand that
healing requires my participation.
My job is to willingly yoke myself to You each day,
trusting that Your yoke is much lighter
than the oppressive burden of unforgiveness.
Admittedly, I am a young, wild ox with a
tendency to want to go my own way.
Lord, please hold me close to You.
Teach me how to forgive others as You have forgiven me.
In the trustworthy, faithful, and forgiving Name
of Jesus Christ, I pray.
Amen.

Shalom
....

I remember it as if it happened just this morning. I plopped down in my big, red chair. Its bulky arms and plush, worn fabric wrapped around me like a bear hug. The aged frame gave way in just the right spots. And God offered His time—quiet, undisturbed time—for me to ponder, pray, and dream with Him.

In that moment, all seemed right with the world. I was at peace, and God had me just where He wanted me. He was about to challenge my trust in Him, by rattling my understanding of peace.

Webster tells us that *peace* is a state of harmony or tranquility. It is the antithesis of contention and strife. But in the Hebrew Scriptures (Old Testament), *peace*, שָׁלוֹם (*shalom*), goes far beyond a quiet moment in a comfy, red chair. For our spiritual ancestors, *shalom* was a state of wholeness found in the presence of God, not in one's circumstances. *Shalom* isn't about chaos-free comfort. It is about confidence in the Lord and trust in His promise to never leave or forsake His children, wherever life takes them. *Shalom* can be found on the highest mountaintops and in the darkest valleys, in still, cool waters as well as fiery, parched deserts.

I first began to understand *shalom* in the wilderness of Israel, the blistering desert that the Israelites had to endure to get to the Promised Land. It's not a place where many tourist groups go; that's a shame. In the summer of 2006, I traveled there with some adventurous folks who wanted to walk not only in the footsteps of Jesus but also in the footsteps of Moses.

"How can anything possibly live out here?" someone asked from somewhere in the middle of our air-conditioned tour bus.

I'll never forget the response from our Israeli guide, Boaz (don't you love his name?). "Nothing can live out here on its own. It's impossible without God," he said. "That's why it's such a special place. To survive here you have to depend on the Lord."

Profound words that rolled around in my mind and heart as we stopped and got out to explore. Under the blazing afternoon sun, I found a quiet spot that looked out over a vast expanse of dusty valleys and striated plateaus. Nothing but dirt and rock formations as far as the eye could see; it took my breath away. *To survive in the wilderness, you have to depend on the Lord.*

> The whole congregation of the sons of Israel grumbled against Moses and Aaron in the wilderness. The sons of Israel said to them, "Would that we had died by the LORD's hand in the land of Egypt, when we sat by the pots of meat, when we ate bread to the full; for you have brought us out into this wilderness to kill this whole assembly with hunger." (Exodus 16:2–3)

Just weeks after the Lord delivered His people from the stranglehold of Pharaoh, the Israelites wanted to turn around and go back to a life of slavery in Egypt. Hot, tired, and hungry, they reasoned that if they were going to die, they would prefer to do so where they could get a good meal.

I shake my head in disbelief at their unbelief. A little discomfort and they forget that their God parted the Red Sea (literally!) to free them from bondage. Why would He do that only to watch them die in the desert?

Yeah, K.D. Why would He do that? Why would He miraculously deliver *you* from the bondage of sin, only to let you waste away in a desert of despair?

> Therefore, having been justified by faith, we have peace with God through our Lord Jesus Christ through whom also we have obtained our introduction by faith into this grace in which we stand; and we exult in hope of the glory of God. And not only this, but we also exult in our tribulations, knowing that tribulation brings about perseverance; and perseverance, proven character; and proven character, hope; and hope does not disappoint, because

the love of God has been poured out within our hearts through the Holy Spirit who was given to us. (Romans 5:1–5)

Peace with God, *shalom*. Carved out of the flesh of Jesus, it is found on the Cross. But it may be best understood in the desert, where God will turn our mourning into dancing if we trust Him.

Not long after that day in the wilderness of Israel, I returned home to my comfortable life in Atlanta and plopped down in my comfy, red chair thinking I knew what peace was. Little did I know that I was about to begin a quest for true peace, and it would be the hardest journey of my life. After four years of grueling seminary studies and five years of painful, fear-filled, grief-stricken, crushingly disappointing life, I think I may finally be starting to understand *shalom*.

As of this writing, the season of suffering that began just months after I graduated from Dallas Theological Seminary has stretched well into its fifth year. As I rounded that five-year mark, overwhelming discouragement and disappointment made the turn with me. *Five years, Lord! Really? Five years of my life spent in this desert of despair! For what, Lord? For what?!*

He responded in that still, quiet voice that I have come to know so well. "For Me, and for you, for Deep End Ministries, for this book, and for those who read it." It was the same Voice that met me on my knees as I sobbed over the loss of the exciting and fun life I once had. The Voice that quieted my fearful heart besieged by night terrors. The Voice that communed with me in the Psalms as I prayed through just about every emotion known to man. The Voice that challenged me in my anger and soothed me in my grief. The Voice that broke through the deafening silence of loneliness and isolation. That Voice—His Voice—never went silent, even in my unbelief. His is the Voice of *Shalom. Peace.*

It's been nearly eleven years since I first traveled to the wilderness and fell in love with its exquisitely barren beauty. Today, after a decade of living in my own wilderness, I can tell you that Boaz was right. *To survive here, you have to depend on God.*

Father God,
I am overwhelmed by Your faithfulness.
You have never left my side, even in my unbelief.

Thank You for getting me out of my comfy, red chair
and rattling (make that violently shaking)
my understanding of shalom.
I love You.
K.D.

Epilogue

February 2017

Fifty. It's the new forty, so I hear. It's only a number, so I've been told. You should be glad you're still alive and kicking, so I've been admonished. My knee-jerk reaction is to drop-kick anyone who minimizes this monumental milestone in my life, which is now less than four months away.

"You don't look anywhere close to fifty, so what's the big deal?" I've been asked. I'll tell you what the big deal is. I am a single, well-educated, independent, accomplished, middle-aged woman, *still* living in my mother's basement with my two cats! And just a few weeks ago, Wyoming temperatures dropped to 18 degrees *below* zero! That's 50 degrees *below freezing*! I don't know what's worse? The fifty on the thermometer or the fifty on the calendar!

I can head to a tropical island to escape the brutal, winter weather (which I am blessed to be able to do in just a few days). But there's no escaping that fifty on the calendar. There's not a beach in the world that can slow down the sands of time. Fifty has been taunting me like the wicked witch's hourglass that terrorized Dorothy in the land of Oz.

OK. Maybe a little melodramatic. But you get what I'm saying. Looking at it from my vantage point in the basement, *I am afraid to turn fifty!* Disappointed to think that I will cross that threshold without my independence, financial security, my own home, and a husband and kids to call my own.

Hey, K.D. Have you read *Would I Really Marry Cat*?!

Oh, that's right, I wrote it. So why am I not living it? The compilation

163

of reflections in this book represents five years of wrestling with the Lord. Every word about disappointment, fear, uncertainty, grief, deception, holidays, peace, praise, and trust came from very real, raw, and sometimes ridiculous encounters with God.

But as odd as it sounds, I don't remember a lot of it. In fact, when I sat down to organize this book, I felt as if I were reading my writing for the first time. I know that sounds strange. But depression and trauma can be murder on our memory. In a way, I see that as God's mercy. And I also see it as God's way of ensuring that He gets all of the glory for this book. He entered into that deep, dark hole of despair with me, and never left my side, like the mysterious fourth man in Nebuchadnezzar's furnace (Daniel 3:25). And He used my love of writing to help me survive and process the most painful season of my life with truth and humor. I had no idea that my therapeutic writings would turn into a book. But He did. In fact, I'm guessing He thought it would make for a pretty good fiftieth birthday present.

Our God is an *awesome* God. After revisiting and reflecting on my season in the basement with Him, I am awestruck by His faithfulness and love for me. The words that I don't remember writing are ministering to my heart and soul in ways that I cannot express. And as the darkness lifts, I am excited to apply the lessons from that deep hole of despair.

Which brings me back to my fiftieth birthday. In the midst of a recent meltdown about it, I thought about what would make this entrance into a new decade tolerable. It's highly unlikely that I will get married, have kids, buy a new home, and build wealth in four months. God did part the Red Sea, so it's not completely out of the realm of possibility. But time to put on my big girl pants and get real.

When I really think about it, there are two things that would make it much easier, and maybe even fun, to cross that half-century threshold. Becoming a first-time published author and celebrating with family and members of my tribe (lifelong, faithful, Christ-loving friends in just about every region of the country).

I can't imagine any better fiftieth birthday present than the opportunity to put my first book into the hands of those who have prayed for me, cried with me, encouraged me, challenged me, and loved me with Christ-like love through the darkest season of my life. Though I've guarded their anonymity, you have read about them in the pages of this book. They're the folks in my dream who told me I shouldn't marry my cat. The people who affirmed that, yes, I am a spiritual hoarder. I was with a few of them when God gave me the choice to weep or reap. And when I saw a selfie stick for the first time, it was tribe members who actually told me what it was. I don't know how many times my tribe had to hear me say, "Happiness seems so far away." But I'm so grateful that they stuck it out to rejoice with me over red poppies and singing livers.

I look forward to spending the first year of my new decade of life delivering my heartfelt thanks to each of them. And it looks like God is going to give me a birthday gift like none other—my first book! So, fifty, here I come! To God be the glory!

As hard as it has been, I consider it a privilege to have shared some of my journey with you. I hope *Would I Really Marry My Cat?!* has tickled your funny bone, encouraged you in the midst of your own struggles, and most of all, inspired you to draw nearer to and go deeper with God through His Word and prayer. He is a good and loving Father who promises to never leave or forsake you, no matter where life takes you. There is no better place to be than in His presence, even in the basement.

Shalom,
K.D.

P.S. For years, I have closed all of my correspondence with "*Shalom*" or "*Peace*." Now that I have shared with you some of my most vulnerable and intimate encounters with the Lord, you know the rest of the story.

Acknowledgments

More than forty thousand words have poured out of my heart onto the previous pages of this book. And yet, as I come to these final comments, I am at a loss for words. How do I adequately express my gratitude to those who have come alongside me on this journey—not only the adventure of writing my first book, but also my spiritual sojourn over the past few years? Through darkness and light, despair and hope, pain and praise, loss and love, God has faithfully and graciously placed people in my life who have blessed me with prayer, support, encouragement, compassion, correction, and accountability.

To my mom and family, thank you for allowing me to shelter in place and for loving me even when you didn't recognize the "me" I once was.

To my dad, how grateful I am to have inherited your gift of storytelling. I love and miss you!

To my "kiddos," Larisa, Iliana, Brooklyn, Kaylee, Elijah, Aiden, and Addison, you are true lights of my life. It is my privilege and joy to be your DeeDah. Sugar. Sugar. Sugar ... always.

To my tribe, your love for the Lord is brilliantly magnified in your loyalty and love for this broken and flawed friend. Thank you for helping me find my laugh again.

To Scott, my fierce warrior and friend, thank you for answering God's call to defend me.

To Nikki and Jill, your honesty, affirmation, and willingness to help me find my way out of the darkness and into a wide open space will impact me for the rest of my life.

To Rebecca and Brenda, I am a published author today because you lovingly offered your time, wisdom, keen eyes, and encouragement to me. Thank you.

To Jenne Acevedo, editor and writing coach extraordinaire (Acevedo Word Solutions LLC, JenneAcevedo.com), my deepest gratitude to you for saying "yes" to the Lord, even when it meant taking on a rule-breaker.

To Augusto "Ace" Silva of BlesseD'Signs (acesosilva@gmail.com), thank you for faithfully and joyfully enduring the design process with me. What a gift you are!

To Jamie, what a fun day it was to literally herd cats together. Thank you for your beautiful photography.

To Rebel and Rangler, how blessed I am to have two of the wackiest and most loving four-legged babies on the planet. Momma loves you!

And above all, to my God. The love of the Father, grace of the Son, and fellowship of the Holy Spirit sustain me with every breath I take. You are my light and my salvation. My truth. My treasure. My hope. My peace. My joy. My life. My love. To You be the glory forever and ever. Amen.

End Notes

Chapter 1

1. Dictionary.com
2. R. Laird Harris, Gleason L. Archer Jr., and Bruce K. Waltke, *Theological Wordbook of the Old Testament* (Chicago: Moody Press, 1999), 761.
3. "New Study Links Facebook To Depression: But Now We Actually Understand Why," *Forbes*, April 8, 2015, https://www.forbes.com/sites/alicegwalton/2015/04/08/new-study-links-facebook-to-depression-but-now-we-actually-understand-why/#328c481d1e6d.
4. "Deion Sanders sums up Cam Newton's ugly press conference perfectly," *Fox Sports*, February 7, 2016, http://www.foxsports.com/nfl/story/carolina-panthers-cam-newton-deion-sanders-sums-ugly-press-conference-perfectly-020716.
5. "Read the inspiring text Cam Newton's mom sent him before the Super Bowl," *USA Today Sports*, February 7, 2016, http://ftw.usatoday.com/2016/02/cam-newton-mom-inspiring-text-super-bowl.

Chapter 2

1. Judson W. Van de Venter. "I Surrender All," 1896.
2. "ALERT: Hours After Paris Attack, ISIS Sent This Horrifying Tweet About American Blood... We NEED Trump," *Conservative Tribune*, http://conservativetribune.com/paris-isis-american-blood/.

Chapter 3

1. ESPN.com
2. ESPN.com

Chapter 4

1. Dalai Lama and Howard Cutler, *The Art of Happiness* (Riverhead, 1998); Daniel Gilbert, *Stumbling on Happiness* (Alfred A. Knopf, 2006); Sonja Lyubomirsky, *The How of Happiness: A New Approach to Getting the Life You Want* (Penguin Books, Reprint Edition, 2008); Rick Hanson, *Hardwiring Happiness: The New Brain Science of Contentment, Calm, and Confidence* (Harmony, 2013); Gretchen Rubin, *The Happiness Project* (Harper Collins Publishers, First Edition, 2012); Karle Moore, *The 18 Rules of Happiness Pocket Guide* (Inspire3 Publishing, Second Edition, 2016).
2. LinkedIn, https://www.linkedin.com/pulse/happiness-work-firoz-sait.
3. Dr. J. Dwight Pentecost, *The Joy of Living* (Kregel Publications, 1996).
4. "Brittany Maynard Slams Doctor's Remarks on Her Decision to Die," *NBC News*, October 23, 2014, http://www.nbcnews.com/health/health-news/brittany-maynard-slams-doctors-remarks-her-decision-die-n232576.
5. "Terminally ill woman tells Brittany Maynard death not 'without beauty,'" *Christian Examiner*, October 29, 2014, http://www.christianexaminer.com/article/two-roads-of-terminal-illness/47534.htm.
6. "Death With Dignity Advocate Brittany Maynard Dies in Oregon," *NBC News*, November 2, 2014, http://www.nbcnews.com/health/health-news/death-dignity-advocate-brittany-maynard-dies-oregon-n235091.
7. Ibid.

Chapter 5

1. "The 25 Best Inventions of 2014," *TIME*, November 19, 2014, http://time.com/3594971/the-25-best-inventions-of-2014/.
2. "World to tourists: Leave the selfie stick at home," *The Christian Science Monitor*, March 12, 2015, http://www.csmonitor.com/Technology/2015/0312/World-to-tourists-Leave-the-selfie-stick-at-home.
3. "Stretch Armstrong," *retroland*, http://www.retroland.com/stretch-armstrong/.

Chapter 6

1. "Poet John McCrae," poets.org, https://www.poets.org/poetsorg/poet/john-mccrae.
2. "In Flanders Fields," poets.org, https://www.poets.org/poetsorg/poem/flanders-fields.

Chapter 7

1. "Man seeks restraining order against God," *The Times of Israel,* May 4, 2016, http://www.timesofisrael.com/man-seeks-restraining -order-against-god/.

Chapter 8

1. *Forrest Gump,* Paramount Pictures, 1994.
2. "Before Kris Jenkins's Shot, There Was Ryan Arcidiacono's Pass," *The New York Times,* April 5, 2016, https://www.nytimes.com/2016/04/06/sports/ ncaabasketball/kris-jenkins-ryan-arcidiacono-villanova.html.
3. "Olympic Winners Boudia, Johnson: 'Our Identity Is in Christ,'" *CBN News,* August 9, 2016, http://www1.cbn.com/cbnnews/us/2016/august/ olympic-winners-boudia-johnson-our-identity-is-in-christ.
4. "Wayde van Niekerk glorifies God after winning men's 400m: 'JESUS DID IT,'" *CHRISTIAN TODAY,* August 15, 2016, http://www.christiantoday.com/ article/wayde.van.niekerk.glorifies.god.after.winning.mens.400m.jesus.did. it/93189.htm.
5. "Track Star Trayvon Bromell: 'Without God, I Wouldn't Be Able to Run,'" *CBN News,* August 12, 2016, http://www1.cbn.com/cbnnews/us/2016/august/ track-star-trayvon-bromell-without-god-i-wouldnt-be-able-to-run.
6. "Olympian who helped competitor who fell: 'God prepared my heart to respond in that way,'" *CHRISTIAN TODAY,* August 18, 2016, http://www. christiantoday.com/article/olympian.who.helped.competitor.who.fell.god. prepared.my.heart.to.respond.in.that.way/93410.htm.

Chapter 9

1. Contactmusic.com
2. Dr. J. Dwight Pentecost, *The Words and Works of Jesus Christ* (Zondervan, 1981).

Printed in the United States
By Bookmasters